Farewell, Jackie

Also by Edward Klein

*The Kennedy Curse: Why Tragedy Has Haunted
America's First Family for 150 Years
Just Jackie: Her Private Years
All Too Human: The Love Story of Jack and Jackie Kennedy*

Novels
*The Parachutists
If Israel Lost the War*
(coauthored with Richard Chesnoff and Robert Littell)

Farewell, Jackie

A PORTRAIT
OF HER
FINAL DAYS

EDWARD KLEIN

Viking

VIKING
Published by the Penguin Group
Penguin Group (USA) Inc., 375 Hudson Street, New York, New York 10014, U.S.A.
Penguin Books Ltd, 80 Strand, London WC2R 0RL, England
Penguin Books Australia Ltd, 250 Camberwell Road, Camberwell,
Victoria 3124, Australia
Penguin Books Canada Ltd, 10 Alcorn Avenue, Toronto, Ontario, Canada M4V 3B2
Penguin Books India (P) Ltd, 11 Community Centre, Panchsheel Park,
New Delhi – 110 017, India
Penguin Books (NZ) Ltd, Cnr Airborne and Rosedale Roads, Albany,
Auckland 1310, New Zealand
Penguin Books (South Africa) (Pty) Ltd, 24 Sturdee Avenue,
Rosebank, Johannesburg 2196, South Africa

Penguin Books Ltd, Registered Offices:
80 Strand, London WC2R 0RL, England

First published in 2004 by Viking Penguin, a member of Penguin Group (USA) Inc.

1   3   5   7   9   10   8   6   4   2

Grateful acknowledgment is made for permission to reprint excerpts from the
following copyrighted works:
"Miss Gee" from the *Collected Poems* by W. H. Auden. Copyright 1940 and renewed
1968 by W. H. Auden. Used by permission of Random House, Inc.
"Ithaka" from *C. P. Cavafy: Collected Poems*, translated by Edmund Keeley and Philip
Sherrard. © 1975 by Edmund Keeley and Philip Sherrard. Reprinted by permission
of Princeton University Press.

Photograph credits appear on pages 211–212.

CIP data available

ISBN 0-670-03331-6

This book is printed on acid-free paper.

Printed in the United States of America
Set in Adobe Garamond
Designed by Erin Benach

For Dolores, who shares many of Jackie's finest qualities, including her dignity, grace, and uncommon common sense

CONTENTS

INTRODUCTION

$\mathcal{J}$acqueline Kennedy Onassis is still so much with us that it is hard to believe she has been gone for ten long years.

Perhaps that is because the blazing klieg lights of attention that pursued Jackie during her lifetime did not forsake her in death. Since May 1994, when she was laid to rest on a hillside in Arlington National Cemetery next to her first husband, President John F. Kennedy, Jackie has been the subject of numerous biographies, countless televised documentaries, two off-Broadway musicals, a made-for-television movie, a frenzied Sotheby's auction, and a traveling exhibition featuring the original gowns, dresses, suits, and accessories she wore during her White House years.

On the tenth anniversary of her death, our desire to know more about Jackie remains insatiable. Practically any morsel, it seems, will do. Recently, for instance, newspapers around the world carried a forty-year-old story reporting that Jackie once briefly considered suicide then quickly put the idea aside.

And yet, despite this intense and unrelenting scrutiny, there have been only the sketchiest accounts of Jackie's final illness and death. That story began on the day Jackie fell from her horse while foxhunting in Virginia, and reached its sad climax when she learned the shocking news that her cancer was incurable. Though her doctors told Jackie they could keep her alive awhile longer, she chose not to pursue any further aggressive medical treatment. All this happened with dizzying swiftness: in six short months Jackie plummeted from the height of personal contentment and professional fulfillment to the threshold of death. How she coped with this calamity is a tale both heart-wrenching and heartwarming.

I have written about Jackie before, both in magazines and in books. Although I did not number myself among Jackie's close friends, I knew her for the last dozen years of her life. We frequently chatted on the phone and lunched together. My wife and I were guests in her home.

Like millions of others, I greatly admired Jackie for her lively, affectionate nature, her dignity and grace. And I deeply respected her decision to orchestrate her own death as masterfully as she once orchestrated the funeral of President Kennedy.

Here is the missing piece of Jackie's remarkable story.

Farewell, Jackie

I

The Real Jackie

November 1993

JBKO at the Piedmont Hunt

*I*t was Saturday, November 20, just before daybreak in the hunt country of Virginia. A solemn darkness enveloped the rolling countryside between historic Llangollen Farm and Ayrshire, north of the village of Upperville. All at once, the gloom was pierced by the sound and lights of a caravan of trucks and SUVs towing big, six-horse vans and smaller two-horse tagalongs. The headlights made a circuit of the surrounding fields, then fell upon a barn, silhouetting it against the sapphire sky. There, a tall, slim woman leaned against the side of the barn, one booted leg casually crossed over the other. She was puffing on a cigarette and exhaling streams of thick smoke into the frigid morning air.

This was Jacqueline Bouvier Kennedy Onassis. She was sixty-four years old, but the years had done nothing to extinguish her incandescent beauty. She was dressed in a handsomely cut black frock coat with a canary yellow collar denoting a member in full standing of the Piedmont Foxhounds. She wore buff-colored breeches with a mild flare at the thigh; a snowy-white stock tied at her throat (to be used as a sling or tourniquet in case of emergency); a black velvet hunt cap; and a pair of white gloves.

Waiting in the dark by the barn, Jackie lit a fresh Pall Mall from the glowing end of the one she had just finished. Few people knew that she chain-smoked when she thought no one was looking. Yet despite all the years of smoking, Jackie's teeth remained sparkling white and her face was radiant with color. Tendrils of thick, dark hair peeked out from her black hunt cap, clinging to her face and accentuating its ethereal, wide-eyed loveliness.

She looked like a woman who cared deeply about her appearance. And, in fact, she swam, rode horses, water-skied, jogged around New York's Central Park Reservoir, and practiced yoga. She kept herself Bouvier-thin on a strict low-calorie diet. Four and a half years before, in the spring of 1989, she had had a face-lift performed by Dr. Michael Hogan, a Park Avenue plastic surgeon.

In addition to smoking, Jackie had another habit of which few people were aware. When she was stressed out, she bit her nails. In the past few years, as she had grown more contented with her life, the compulsive bouts of finger-gnawing became rarer and rarer. But on the weekend before Thanksgiving—which usually coincided with the weekend before the anniversary of John F. Kennedy's assassination—Jackie bit her fingernails to the quick.

This year, her anxiety level seemed higher than ever, for 1993 marked a major milestone; it was the thirtieth anniversary of the assassination. The event filled Jackie with dread, not only because of the gruesome images that were engraved in her memory of that bloody Friday in Dallas, but also because all the media hoopla stirred up painful recollections of her difficult marriage to Jack Kennedy.

While others celebrated JFK's virtues, Jackie could not help but be reminded of the humiliations she endured at the hands of her philandering husband. Even worse, the anger and rage she had felt toward Jack Kennedy while he was still alive surfaced at assassination-anniversary time, threatening to overwhelm her.

Invariably, Jackie would experience terrible pangs of guilt because of these spiteful feelings toward her now-dead husband. And the guilt would sometimes become almost unbearable when she thought back, as she did every November, to the final months leading up to Jack's death, when their relationship was undergoing a profound change.

By the fall of 1963, a strong new bond had developed between Jack and Jackie as a result of their shared experiences in the White House and their grief over the death of their two-day-old son Patrick Bouvier. Jack was far more considerate of Jackie's feelings; for the first time anyone could remember, he held Jackie's hand in public when they disembarked from Air Force One at Love Field in Dallas. For her part, Jackie was more in love with Jack than at any time since he had become president.

This new tenderness explained why Jackie, who hated campaigning, agreed to go with Jack on a political fence-mending trip to Texas in November 1963. It also explained why, each year at this time, Jackie would have given anything to erase the crushing guilt she bore for having once harbored such hostile feelings toward Jack.

o o o o o o

In the gathering dawn of the Virginia countryside, members of the Piedmont Foxhounds arrived at the meet site and greeted Jackie. (She was called JBKO by her hunt friends, but never to her face.) The women were dressed in black like Jackie, but the men were turned out in a more spectacular fashion. They wore scarlet frock coats, well-polished black boots with brown tops, loosely cut white breeches, white gloves, and black velvet helmets. Some had on spurs and carried long-thonged whips.

Jackie's friends in Virginia did not fawn over her the way people tended to do elsewhere. Here in the hunt country, she was not treated as a celebrity. Her fellow equestrians admired her for her horsemanship. That Jackie hunted with Piedmont—a club famous for its speed, big fences, tough hunters, and daring—was testimony to her personal devotion to the sport.

"She was a serious, serious rider," said one of Jackie's hunting friends, Barbara Graham, who was an heir to the Johnson & Johnson wax fortune. "Jackie was forever quizzing me on how I did things with my horses. She wanted to know everything. We'd talk for hours on my porch."

Jackie's love of horses started at an early age. As a child of six, she began schooling in dressage—the art of controlling a horse with subtle movements of the hands, legs, and weight. She kept a horse at Miss Porter's, the boarding school she attended in Farmington, Connecticut. It was her Vassar classmate Gay Estin who encouraged her to get a hunt box—a weekend house with a small barn and paddock—in Virginia.

Recently, Jackie had written a foreword to James L. Young's *A Field of Horses: The World of Marshall P. Hawkins,* a coffee-table book about the equestrian photographer who had taken a famous picture of her in 1961 falling headfirst from her horse when it balked at a fence. Of hunting in the open country, Jackie wrote: "As we see them [horses and riders] move together across the exquisite landscapes, we are made aware of our own responsibilities to preserve and conserve the simple splendor of a vanishing America."

o o o o o o

This weekend, Jackie was a guest at Rokeby Farm, the estate of her lifelong friends Paul Mellon, the renowned art collector, philanthropist, and horseman, and Rachel Lambert "Bunny" Mellon. There were no fewer than ten foxhunt clubs within an hour's drive of the Mellons' 4,200-acre farm. Jackie hunted with the two most exclusive—the Orange County Hunt and the Piedmont Foxhounds.

Rokeby was located in Piedmont territory, just to the west of Orange County territory. The Masters of the Foxhounds Association in nearby Leesburg controlled the hunts, and kept track of which land went with which hunt. Because there were so many hunt clubs, it was important to know where one ended and another began. In the case of the Piedmont Foxhounds and the Orange County Hunt, the line was known, tongue in cheek, as Segregation Lane. The only time a Piedmont hunt was allowed to go into Orange County territory was when the fox and hounds crossed Segregation Lane and the riders had no choice but to follow.

Because the area had more manicured grasslands than rough crop fields, it was considered ideal for hunting. To keep out the riffraff, the best clubs had a policy that members had to own at least one hundred acres of land. Guests of the members were allowed to hunt three times a year by paying a "capping" fee of two hundred dollars per hunt—a holdover term from English days when a rider placed his daily fee in a hunt servant's cap.

To its devotees like Jackie, foxhunting was more passion than sport. As the hunting expert Mason Houghland wrote in *Gone Away:* "It is a religion, a faith; in it are all the elements that form the framework upon which beliefs are built: the attempt to escape from life as it is to life as we would have it; an abiding love of beauty; and an unconscious search for the eternal verities of fair play, loyalty and sympathetic accord, which are so clouded in our mundane existence."

o o o o o o

The sky over eastern Virginia began to lighten, and the horses were unloaded from the vans. Plumes of vapor issued from their nostrils. Jackie was not riding her favorite horse, Frank, with whom she had won the hunter trials at the Orange County Hunt three years before. Instead, she had chosen to ride a dark bay Thoroughbred gelding (a castrated male horse) who had once raced over hurdles, but who now, in his later years, was happy to follow the hounds.

It was not clear to Jackie's fellow riders why she had switched mounts. Was Frank disabled? Did Jackie seek the challenge provided by an unfamiliar horse? Whatever her reason, Jackie's decision to ride a strange horse (a fact that has never been reported until now) set off a rapid chain of events that began with her fall from the horse and ended six months later with her death.

Piedmont's chief huntsman, Randy Waterman, nodded hello to Jackie. Waterman was responsible for the territory, the fences, the horses, and the hounds—for everything that went with providing sport to the paid subscribers. He was well known for his "surprise" method of foxhunting.

"There are basically two theories about foxhunting," explained Betsy Parker, who covered equestrian sports for a chain of papers in rural and northern Virginia. "In one method, you go out quietly, slowly, walking up to places where foxes might be found—little woodlands, low-lying grassy areas, anywhere the huntsman thinks he will find a fox—and the fox will eventually hear your approach and move away, sometimes at a trot, sometimes, depending on scenting conditions, at a mad dash—and the hunt is on.

"The other method," she continued, "is the gallop-up-to-the-covert and surprise the heck out of Mr. Reynard,* to get him on the move quickly. That was Randy Waterman's choice, which made for basically running and jumping from the get-go, all day, all the time."

One of the grooms, Leroy Moore, helped Jackie mount. Her horse had a freshly braided mane and tail, and gleamed with health and care. The frozen dew covering the ground squealed and

*Renard, a fox, is the hero of the French medieval-beast epic *Roman de Renart*.

crackled beneath the hooves of the horses. The smell of snow was in the air. It was going to be a perfectly horrible day—cold, damp, and dark. Ideal hunting weather for the scent-sniffing hounds. And a day made to order for Jackie.

The real Jackie.

The Jackie most people rarely got to see.

o o o o o o

There was no resemblance between Jackie in the flesh and the woman people read about in slander-mongering books and supermarket tabloids. That woman was a figment of the media's imagination, a creature who had been invented by sensational journalists following Jackie's highly unpopular marriage in 1968 to Greek shipping tycoon Aristotle Onassis.

Millions of Americans saw the marriage as a betrayal of trust. They had expected Jackie to remain forever on display like a piece of Royal Dresden—delicate and untouchable. When she fell off her pedestal into the arms of a dark, lecherous foreigner, people stopped viewing her as an object of uncritical devotion. The once-saintly icon was transformed, practically overnight, into a greedy, grasping witch nicknamed Jackie O.

Her detractors were not confined to the tabloid press or to stand-up comedians like Joan Rivers, who asked the women in her Las Vegas audience: "Come on, be honest, would you sleep with Onassis? Do you believe she does? Well, she has to do something. I mean, you can't stay in Bergdorf's shopping all day."

The Vatican got into the act, too. It considered the idea of excommunicating Jackie, then thought better of it. But the Vatican announced that Jackie would no longer be eligible to receive the sacraments of the Holy Church, because she had married a divorced man.

After Onassis died in 1975, Jackie was automatically eligible again to receive the sacraments of the Church. But almost fifteen years after his death, Jackie was still struggling to cleanse her reputation of the tabloid sludge. In 1989, C. David Heymann's bestselling biography *A Woman Named Jackie* drew a devastating picture of a shallow woman who was obsessed with the material side of life.

Jackie's friends wondered why she wasn't more effective in combating this distorted stereotype. Perhaps the answer lay in her guilty conscience. Strange as it might sound, Jackie sometimes wondered in the presence of friends if she *did* deserve all the scorn that was being heaped upon her.

As she once told Onassis's sister Artemis: "Sometimes I think that I am responsible for my misfortune. My first husband died in my arms. I was always telling him that he should be protected, but he would not listen to me. Before my second husband died, I was always telling him to take care of himself, but he wouldn't listen to me [either]."

Her friends in Virginia did not recognize Jackie in the media's portrayal of her as a cold, calculating she-monster. They knew her as a tender, warm, and witty woman.

"It's queer how her public persona and her real self are so unalike," former ambassador to Thailand Charles Whitehouse told the author of this book in 1989, long before Jackie had begun to receive proper credit for her affiliation with the arts, the preservation movement, and the John F. Kennedy Library. "I've given a lot of thought to this, and I think it's because she hasn't become connected in the public mind with any virtuous cause. She's not perceived like Lady Bird Johnson, planting and making things beautiful, or like Barbara Bush with reading. And, you know, being involved with a national problem might have eased Jackie's situation.

"So why doesn't she just do it?" he continued. "It may be connected in some way with her being fiercely independent and not willing to be involved superficially in something just for the sake of the press. Jackie is clearly not gripped by children with rickets. What she is, is a fascinating, somewhat perplexing human being—lively, sporty, affectionate, youthful. Not at all like the acquisitive monster that is portrayed in the press."

o o o o o o

"The heavy gray November sky couldn't decide whether to spit snow or rain," recalled one of Jackie's hunting friends.

Jackie and Barbara Graham, along with a field of fifty other riders, moved off, following the hounds, a well-matched pack with white bodies marked with black and brown patches and spots. The hounds dove eagerly into a wooded thicket. They soon found the scent of the fox and were off—tails waving, noses down, howling furiously. Unlike foxhunting in England, the goal of the sport in America was not to kill the creature, just to chase it.

The thundering hooves, the music of the hounds in full cry, and the hunters' horn echoed through the Shenandoah Valley and off the wooded hills. The riders followed closely behind the field master, taking a hefty wall, trying to keep up with the tumbling pack. The countryside was laced with old stone walls and tall post-and-beam chestnut fences, which had been milled before the great chestnut blight at the turn of the twentieth century.

Breathing heavily with excitement, perspiring despite the freezing cold, the riders entered a wooded area, then streamed out of it, one by one, and faced another old stone wall just behind historic Trinity Episcopal Church in Upperville. Several of the riders were having trouble negotiating the small wall.

"It was starting to fall down," recalled Barbara Graham. "There were rocks littering the ground in front of it. It wasn't a great approach, so I turned my horse left, riding down the line, to look for a better place to jump."

Barbara glanced over her shoulder to see if Jackie was still with her. But Jackie had fallen back. She was separated by several horses from Barbara, and did not see her friend turn away to find a better jumping spot.

"Jackie's horse took off well back from the wall," Barbara said. "He was trying to avoid the fallen stones, I guess. He basically landed on his nose, and she catapulted right over his head."

Jackie hit the ground with a loud thud.

"Oh, my God!" screamed a spectator, "she must have broken her neck."

Barbara and another friend of Jackie's, Ann Tate, instantly dismounted and rushed to Jackie's side, while other riders caught up with her loose horse. The rest of the field streamed away, following the screaming pack of hounds.

"Later, I called Mrs. Mellon and told her what had happened," Barbara said. "I told her that Jackie was unconscious for thirty minutes."

Like many experienced riders, Jackie had taken spills before. As a young woman, she had fallen off a horse and was semiconscious for three days. But today's fall was particularly bad. The accident appeared to be caused by a number of factors other than the condition of the stone wall. To begin with, she was riding an unfamiliar horse who was not entirely under her control during the fast and furious jumps required in the Piedmont-style of hunting. In addition, she seemed to lose her focus at the very moment her horse took off over the wall, perhaps because her mind was on other things. Finally, looking back from the perspective of what we now know about Jackie's health in the fall of 1993, she was clearly in no condition to ride that day.

"I got a call about Jackie from one of her friends who also hap-

pened to be my patient," said Dr. Bernard Kruger, a well-known New York cancer specialist. "This patient told me about Jackie's accident, and I said, 'It doesn't sound as though she fell off her horse by accident. If I were her, I'd be concerned about what's going on with my health.'"

A WORLDLY HUNGER

$\mathscr{I}$ was home when my pager went off," recalled Sheila Sisk, a member of the Middleburg Volunteer Fire and Rescue Squad. "It said: 'injury from fall from horse.' I immediately drove to the fire-house, where they told us the accident had occurred behind the Episcopal Church in Upperville. When we got there, the rider was still on the grass, but she had regained consciousness, and was sitting up."

Barbara Graham and Ann Tate were kneeling on the soft turf next to Jackie, tending to their friend. The two women did not seem overly concerned, perhaps because such falls were common during hunts. The arrival of the emergency rescue squad—a frequent sight in Upperville during the hunting season—drew only a handful of curious spectators.

"I'm perfectly fine," Jackie said when Sheila approached.

As Sheila later recalled, she instantly recognized that her injured patient was the most famous woman in the world. On the spot, she decided to treat Jackie as she would any other accident victim. She insisted on taking Jackie's pulse and her other vital signs, and hooking her up to oxygen. Then she and two other volunteers strapped Jackie to a backboard and loaded her into an ambulance for the ride to the Loudoun Memorial Hospital Center in Leesburg.

"She was in some pain," said Jerry Embrey, captain of the Middleburg Rescue Squad, "but I think she was in shock more than anything else. For a lady of her years to have taken such a fall and come through pretty much unscathed is almost a miracle."

At the hospital, Jackie was examined by Bunny Mellon's physician. He was impressed by Jackie's remarkable physical condition and could find little wrong with her, except for some minor swelling in her groin that seemed to be caused by a swollen lymph node. He diagnosed it as an infection and prescribed antibiotics.

oooooo

By the next morning, Sunday, November 21, the swelling had gone down, and Jackie was released from the hospital. Her accident was treated so lightly by the doctors that the media hardly paid notice. The Associated Press mentioned the incident in a brief, five-sentence item.

Jackie's close friend Bunny picked her up in an immaculately restored vintage Mercedes-Benz sedan and took her back to Rokeby Farm, the Mellon estate in Upperville.

Bunny's husband, Paul Mellon, was described by one writer as having been "richer longer than any other man in America." He was worth more than eight hundred million dollars. He had a brilliant eye for art and had been the chief benefactor of the National Gallery of Art in Washington, D.C., for the past several decades.

Jackie was impressed by the Mellons' wealth and their style of life. Money—and the protective veneer it provided—had always been important to her. After her parents divorced in 1940 (when Jackie was eleven years old) and her mother remarried, to Hugh D.

Auchincloss, Jackie and her sister, Lee, lived at Merrywood, the large Auchincloss estate in McLean, Virginia. The Auchinclosses came from a long line of WASP blue bloods, while Jackie's forebears on both her mother's and father's sides came from Catholic working-class immigrants who had invented an aristocratic pedigree for themselves. What's more, while "Hughdie" Auchincloss's five children were in line to receive comfortable trust funds from their grandmother, who was an heir to the Standard Oil fortune, Jackie and Lee had no inheritance of which to speak.

Like many world-famous celebrities who have had hard-luck childhoods, Jackie always felt that she was a bit of an imposter and that someone would eventually find her out. She dreamed of a life insulated by luxury.

The Mellons' Rokeby Farm provided that insulation—and then some. It had its own jet landing strip. The walls of the main house, called Oak Springs Farm, were hung with priceless paintings. There was a magnificent Pissarro in the guest bath. The library boasted a collection of rare books illuminated by William Blake. A separate structure called the Brick House was filled with Paul's English sporting art. Bunny's garden library, one of the most important repositories on the history of horticulture, was housed in a handsome stone building designed by architect Edward Larabee Barnes. The stables were filled with the finest Thoroughbred bloodstock, including Paul's horse, Snow Goose.

But what impressed Jackie most of all was that nothing about Rokeby or its appointments was ostentatious. Bunny saw to that. Among the style cognoscenti, her taste was considered to be unsurpassed. As Jackie said, "Bunny has a genius for creating an atmosphere of rarified luxury without a hint of vulgarity."

Everything in Bunny's home was understated—the furniture, the slipcovers, the curtains, the carpets. It was all so restrained that it made a visitor almost forget that the paintings on the walls were some of the greatest works of art in the world.

Jackie's favorite story about Bunny's single-minded devotion to perfectionism concerned how Bunny picked the color for the living room in her house on the grounds of the exclusive Mill Reef Club in Antigua.

"I was trying to describe to my interior decorator the salmon-pink color that I had in mind," Bunny said. "And I simply told him, 'You know how it is when you get up at five o'clock in the morning, and go into your garden, and the sun is coming up? Well, it's not the color of the light on the first petal of the rose. And it's not the color when you pull off the second petal. It's the color on the third petal. That's what I'm trying to achieve!'"

Besides Oak Springs Farm and Antigua, Bunny was the mistress of several other houses—a brick mansion on Washington's Embassy Row, a French-style town house in New York City, a vacation home in Nantucket, and an apartment on the Avenue Foch in Paris.

"Bunny runs the houses beautifully," said a frequent guest, who was quoted by the art critic Martin Filler in his article, "Cool Mellon," in the April 1992 issue of *Vanity Fair*. "It's the best. Usually, it's a group of four or five [guests] at the most. And you're surrounded by smiling faces who want to do things for you. She's got people who have been there thirty years, and she's always seen that everything is perfect."

Jackie saw a reflection of herself in Bunny, who hid an iron fist inside her velvet glove.

"The words commonly used to describe [Jackie's] beauty— 'shimmering,' 'ethereal'—reinforce the impression of her other-worldliness," wrote an acquaintance of Jackie's, the author Judith Thurman. "There was plenty of worldly hunger in Jackie, and steeliness, too. One sees it in her carriage. But these were sheathed, like the nails she bit to the quick, by the white gloves she wore even when she was perched atop an elephant in the heat of India, by her decorous reserve, her wifely deference, and the 'feathery' voice that seemed never to utter an arrogant, vulgar, or impolitic word. In private, though, she could be impious, even wicked. And those who knew her well also knew that, like the most absolute of queens, she was swift to punish, with implacable disfavor, the perceived crime of lèse-majesté."

Jackie and Bunny spent hours going through Bunny's huge closets, which contained several hundred thousand dollars' worth of Hubert de Givenchy's entire haute couture line for the season. When the topic wasn't clothes, they chatted about horticulture (Bunny was a world-class expert on the subject), or interior design, or how things should look in a house.

"Nothing," said Bunny, "should be noticed."

o o o o o o

Jackie and Bunny were soul mates, and to understand one was to understand the other.

As children, both suffered from painful shyness and a lack of self-esteem. Bunny's father, the Listerine mouthwash tycoon Gerard Barnes Lambert, sent Bunny to a psychotherapist, who prescribed a behavior-modification program to help her overcome her timidity. She was ordered to stand in front of a mirror and tell herself over and over, "You are wonderful, and beautiful, and the most glamorous young lady in the world, the most wonderful, the prettiest young woman."

Jackie, for her part, was emotionally scarred by her parents' venomous marriage. But unlike Bunny's sessions of self-reinforcement, her therapy was reading.

"I read a lot when I was little," she said, "much of which was too old for me. There were Chekhov and Shaw in the room where I had to take naps, and I never slept but sat on the windowsill reading, then scrubbed the soles of my feet so the nurse would not see I had been out of bed. My heroes were Byron, Mowgli, Robin Hood, Little Lord Fauntleroy's grandfather, and Scarlett O'Hara."

Sometimes, Jackie and Bunny talked about their shyness and how it had crippled their lives.

"You know," Jackie said, "I've had to get over being shy and timid, because it doesn't appear to be normal to other people. It's very uncomfortable and painful for me to have to put myself forward, but I've learned to do it, and it works. It's a big mistake thinking that being deferential is going to be perceived as good manners. People don't understand it. It's going to be perceived as not being in control of what's going on."

But perhaps what cemented the relationship between Jackie and Bunny more than anything else was the similarity of their marriages. Both women had learned to deal with their husbands' unfaithfulness.

"Women who share that kind of problem—straying husbands— have a kind of unspoken understanding," said Robin Duke, whose own husband, Angier Biddle Duke, was chief of protocol during the Kennedy administration. "It is a subtle part of their relationship. But it's important, because women like Bunny and Jackie learn how to cope, how to share their husbands with other women, and it ultimately changes their entire attitude toward life."

While Jackie was first lady, she sought Bunny's artistic advice and financial support for many of her most notable projects, including the restoration of the White House, and the lavish state dinners attended by world-famous artists. Among other things, Bunny created the sublime White House Rose Garden. After the assassination in Dallas, it was Bunny who helped Jackie review films and photos of historic funerals. And it was Bunny who came up with the idea of using a riderless horse for President Kennedy's funeral procession.

For months, while Jackie languished in a deep depression and

could hardly function, Bunny assumed the role of her guardian and protector. She showered Jackie with lavish presents: a five-thousand-dollar Schlumberger bracelet from Tiffany & Co., a seventeen-thousand-dollar bed crafted by Bunny's own ironmonger, the use of the Mellons' private Gulfstream jet.

When Jackie bought a home in Martha's Vineyard, she asked Bunny to supervise its decoration, both inside and out. Bunny designed the long, bumpy road leading to Jackie's house, which has since become famous in design circles.

"That road doesn't compete with the wild landscape," said a frequent visitor. "It's just a little bit of a manicured sort of carpet that the house sits on, but then it immediately reverts to the bushy, wild Martha's Vineyard seaside landscape. Bunny also designed the beautiful forecourt that you drive into when you visit Jackie. All that is very shorthanded, and very cool."

However, like most pleasant things in life, Bunny's largesse came with a price.

"[Bunny] desperately needs her court and total control," a New York socialite told Martin Filler. "Once she takes a shine to you, she's terribly, terribly nice and thoughtful and gives presents. But it's sort of cannibalistic. Unless you're careful, she'd like to buy you. . . ."

○○○○○○

Now, as Bunny drove Jackie from the hospital in Leesburg to the farm in Upperville, she attempted to persuade her friend to put off her return to New York City. She wanted Jackie to stay and recuperate for the next few days at Oak Springs Farm. Bunny would see to it that Jackie was properly taken care of. She would look after everything. Bunny would take charge.

In the past, Jackie would never have used the word *no* with Bunny. But Jackie was no longer a helpless, clinging, dependent woman. In recent years, she had become a self-confident personality who radiated a swelling self-assurance. She felt strong and secure enough to disappoint her best friend.

As they pulled up in front of Oak Springs Farm, Jackie explained that she had responsibilities to attend to back in New York. She did not have to remind Bunny that tomorrow was the bleakest day in the Kennedy calendar: the anniversary of John F. Kennedy's assassination.

THE CROSS SHE HAD TO BEAR

----

*T*he next morning, Monday, November 22, Jackie flew back to New York in the Mellons' Gulfstream II, whose interior was decorated like a men's club with dark woods, brown plaids, and corduroy. As the plane prepared to land at the Marine Air Terminal at La Guardia Airport in Queens, Jackie crossed herself and buckled her seat belt.

She was still feeling sore from her accident, which she tried to dismiss as just one of those "little things" that happened in foxhunting. She thought of herself as a fit and keen athlete who would not be deterred by a mishap. She planned to get back on a horse as soon as possible.

First, however, she had to recover from the fall. The trouble was, her whole body ached, as though she was coming down with the flu. Perhaps the stress of the anniversary of the assassination had lowered her immunity and made her susceptible to infection. She had no idea that what she was feeling were the first signs of an illness that would consume her life and prevent her from ever mounting a horse again.

ooooooo

A chauffeured car was waiting for her at the airport, and she was driven directly to the Upper East Side of Manhattan. There, every year on this day for the past thirty years, Jackie had organized a requiem mass for her husband at St. Thomas More, a small Catholic church on East Eighty-ninth Street between Madison and Park Avenues.

"The day before the mass," recalled Monsignor George Bardes, then the senior pastor of St. Thomas More, "a message was given to me that a stranger was asking which mass the Kennedys would attend the next day. The stranger was pointed out to me and I didn't like the looks of this guy. So I called the police department and told them that someone was inquiring about the Kennedys. They sent cops."

Jackie and her children, Caroline and John, were frequently the prey of deranged people. In the past couple of weeks alone there had been two frightening incidents: a woman was seized and taken to the psychiatric ward in Bellevue Hospital after stalking Jackie; and a man, packing a .44-caliber pistol and a box of hollow-point bullets, was arrested after trying to deliver a manuscript to Jackie's weekend house in New Jersey.

The files of the New York Police Department bulged with threats of murder, kidnapping, and other forms of mayhem aimed at the Kennedys. Since Jackie and her children were no longer eligible for Secret Service protection, they tried to be careful in their movements around the city. However, when a threat was deemed serious enough, they accepted bodyguards provided by the police.

The most vigilant member of the family was Caroline Kennedy Schlossberg, who had recently turned thirty-six and was married to Edwin Schlossberg, a man thirteen years her senior. Once a pudgy, frumpy teenager, Caroline had turned out to be a thin, attractive woman. She had been the target of several stalker scares over the years, and now that she had three children of her own to look after—Rose, five; Tatiana, three; and a newborn son named Jack—Caroline had chosen to live an extremely secluded, almost reclusive life. She, Ed, and their children, who resided on Park Avenue not far from Jackie's apartment, were rarely seen in public.

By contrast, her brother, John, now thirty-three, and recently named by *People* magazine as "The Sexiest Man Alive," seemed to be everywhere—bicycling through Manhattan traffic, riding the subway, playing touch football in Central Park, on the town with his movie-star girlfriend Daryl Hannah. John had recently quit his job as an assistant district attorney and had started a company with his friend Michael Berman. They called their company Random Ventures, which seemed especially appropriate, for John's life lacked a regular plan, purpose, or pattern. His random life was one of Jackie's biggest concerns.

When Caroline, John, and their mother arrived at St. Thomas

More, the suspicious stranger who had worried Monsignor Bardes was nowhere to be seen. But police snipers were stationed on the roofs of the adjacent buildings, and a couple of police cars were parked in front of the church.

Taking turns, Jackie, Caroline, and John dipped their fingers in the holy water, made the sign of the cross, and genuflected in the direction of the small altar. Behind the altar was a large gold cross, minus the figure of Jesus, an odd omission in a Catholic church.

There was an explanation for the missing Christ figure. The Church of St. Thomas More had been used for a number of years by the Dutch Reformed Church before it was turned over to the Catholic Archdiocese of New York. The inside of the church was an intimate space with neo-Gothic decorations, and it had none of the grandeur of most Catholic houses of worship. The stations of the cross—scenes of Christ's suffering on the path to his crucifixion—ringed the church in rustic wood carvings.

Jackie and her children entered the Foley Chapel, a little architectural gem on the west side of the church. Monsignor Bardes was waiting for them there, dressed in black vestments—black representing the color of greatest grief in the Roman Catholic tradition. Jackie's brother-in-law, Senator Edward M. Kennedy, was seated in the front, along with many members of the Kennedy clan. Off in a corner, sitting by herself, was a nun in black habit.

"An old nun named Quigley asked me if she could attend the mass," Monsignor Bardes said. "'Father, I'd like to go into the chapel. After all, I had John in class. I'd like to go in and pray with them.' I told her all right. Later, I explained to Jackie the reason I had given the sister permission to be in the chapel.

"And Jackie said, 'Oh, I'm so glad that sister is here.' And I said, 'Yes, she had John in class.' Jackie called John over and says, 'Father said this nun had you in class, John.' And John takes one look at the nun and says, 'Sorry, but I was never in class with her.'

Apparently this old nun had made up the story about John so that she could later say she had prayed with the Kennedys."

Years later, in an interview with the author of this book, Monsignor Bardes still had a vivid memory of Jackie's reaction to this incident with the deceitful nun. Jackie visibly recoiled when she realized that the nun had managed to slip through the protective cordon erected by the police, and penetrate the intimate gathering of Kennedys. What if the nun had not been a nun at all, but someone in disguise who was bent on doing Jackie and her children harm? What if the "nun" had been an assassin?

"Jackie wasn't the only one who was worried about someone in the disguise of a nun or a priest getting into the church," Monsignor Bardes said. "It was everyone's nightmare."

When she had regained her equilibrium, Jackie walked slowly down the narrow aisle, which was flanked by beautiful stained-glass windows. After she was comfortably seated, Monsignor Bardes began the mass.

"*Ego sum resurrectio et vita. . . .*"

The anniversary of John Kennedy's martyrdom arrived each year near Advent, the period observed by many Christians as a season of prayer and fasting. On the rare occasions when Jackie mentioned Jack's assassination to friends, she expressed the opinion that Lee Harvey Oswald had not acted alone. She believed there had been a conspiracy.

Jackie never explained why she embraced the conspiracy theory, but to those who knew her well, her reasoning was not that difficult to decipher. A well-conceived, expertly carried out plot had a far greater chance of success than the impulsive act of a single, deranged gunman.

Any number of people, acting on their own, might have thwarted a single assassin—the driver of the presidential limousine, the Secret Service agents running beside the car, or Jackie herself.

One of her friends recalled a conversation with Jackie many years after the assassination.

"She was still blaming herself," said the friend. "She said, 'If only I had insisted on a bubbletop. If only I had turned to my right sooner. If only I had done something to save him.' And I asked her, 'What could you have done to save him?' But she didn't have an answer."

The question was unanswerable.

It was the cross Jackie had to bear.

". . . *Non morietur in aeternam . . .*"

Light streamed through the old stained-glass windows.

Newport, Rhode Island
September 12, 1953
(Forty years earlier)

Standing in the entrance hall of St. Mary's Church in Newport, Rhode Island, Jackie examines herself in a mirror and decides that the wedding gown she is wearing does absolutely nothing for her.

Its portrait neckline and fitted bodice emphasize her flat chest and long waist. With her impeccable taste, Jackie would never have chosen such a dress on her own. She would have picked something more sculptural and modern. Something that would have emphasized her long neck, not her long waist.

But Jack Kennedy insisted that she wear a traditional gown. And although Jackie told him that she really, really, *really* didn't like this gown, Jack got his way.

And so now, Jackie is dressed in this horrid gown, which she hates. She tries to fluff up the bouffant skirt with its ridiculous

orange-blossom sprigs coming out of the center of rosettes. She is being fussed over by her sister, Lee, the matron of honor, and her bridesmaids, who are so excited they can't stand still and stop chattering.

This is supposed to be the happiest day of Jackie's life. She is twenty-four years old, and in the next few minutes, she will become the wife of a handsome, enormously rich United States senator who has ambitions to become president. People will call her Mrs. John Fitzgerald Kennedy. Maybe someday they'll call her first lady.

But Jackie is not at all happy. And it is not just the wedding dress that distresses her. In the next few seconds, when the band strikes up the traditional "Wedding March," and she walks down the aisle, she will be on the arm of her stepfather, Hugh Auchincloss. Not on the arm of her father, John Bouvier.

Jackie's mother, Janet, claims that her father is not fit to perform this duty because he is too drunk.

"How drunk is he?" asks Jackie for the umpteenth time.

"Drunk," Janet replies.

"It's all your fault," Jackie says. "You humiliated Daddy by excluding him from all the prenuptial dinner parties. No wonder he got drunk."

Janet tries to interrupt, but Jackie will not let her.

"You couldn't stand it when Daddy attended Lee's wedding and gave her away," Jackie says. "You tried to stop Daddy from coming to Newport. You only care about what people say—how they'll compare Daddy to Uncle Hughdie."

"I will not permit Jack Bouvier to attend the wedding!" Janet says, raising her voice.

In fact, Janet has secretly assigned Lee's husband, Michael Canfield, to get her former husband so intoxicated that he cannot make it out of his hotel room and to the wedding. She has been assured by Michael that he has been successful in his mission, and that Jack Bouvier is out cold.

And so, the march down the aisle proceeds as Janet intends, without Jack Bouvier.

After the Most Reverend Richard J. Cushing, Archbishop of Boston, proclaims the couple man and wife, Jackie and Jack kiss. It is a heady moment, and they turn and walk toward the church door, smiling and nodding to friends and relatives.

As Jackie approaches the back of the church, something catches her eye. It is the figure of a man with shiny black hair, sitting next to Jack's friend Charles Spalding. The man's eyes glisten with tears.

It takes Jackie a moment to realize that this is her father. She is thoroughly confused. She thought her father was too drunk to leave his hotel room. What is he doing here among the spectators? If he is sober, why didn't he come to the church in time to walk her down the aisle?

All at once, Jackie understands what has happened. Her

mother lied to her. Her father was never too drunk to perform his duty. And he certainly is not too drunk now. He could have given her away.

The doors to the church open, and light floods inside, blinding Jackie for a moment. She can hear shouts and screams coming from the thousands of people outside St. Mary's Church, straining behind police barricades to get a glimpse of the dashing United States senator and his beautiful new wife.

Jackie feels too sorry for her father to feel sorry for herself.

II

An Incongruous Couple

December 1993

JACKIE, JOHN, AND MAURICE

*I*t was a chilly Saturday in late December, about a month since Jackie's hunting accident. She and her two oldest grandchildren, Rose and Tatiana, attended a matinee performance of *The Nutcracker,* then went shopping at Bergdorf Goodman. "Grand Jackie," as her grandchildren called her, bought presents for everybody, including the girls' classmates at Brearly, the private school they attended, and "Uncle Maurice." Maurice Tempelsman, the Belgian-born diamond merchant, was the man with whom Jackie had been living for the past dozen years.

Normally, Christmas was not Jackie's favorite holiday. As the child of divorce, she did not have many happy memories of Christmases in New York City. But this year was different. Several months before, Caroline had given birth to a boy, and named him John Bouvier, after both her father and her maternal grandfather. Grand Jackie was looking forward to opening presents on Christmas morning with her grandchildren. She had no idea that she stood on a precipice. She was about to fall from the height of happiness and contentment into a well of suffering and discontent: a terrible illness, brutal treatments, and the very real prospect of death.

○○○○○○

In her gay mood, Jackie loaded up her BMW with dozens of colorfully wrapped Christmas presents, squeezed behind the wheel, and headed for her country house in Peapack, New Jersey, where she planned to celebrate the holiday with her family. The large house, which was set on ten beautiful acres of rolling hills, had seven bedrooms—more than enough room for everyone. Maurice and the kids would follow shortly, each in his or her own car.

As Jackie later recalled the drive along Route 287, she slipped a tape into the player, and listened to her friend Carly Simon accompany Frank Sinatra in a selection from his latest album, *Duets.* Jackie chain-smoked as she drove, and when she tried to sing along with "In the Wee Small Hours of the Morning," she suddenly gagged on the smoke and had to pull off onto the shoulder of the road and stop.

Since her hunting accident, she had been feeling clammy, rundown, and fatigued. She often found herself out of breath. Maurice urged her to see a doctor. But Jackie did not think she was sick enough for that. She had not been seriously ill since 1964, when a sinus infection put her briefly in the hospital. Like most chronically healthy people, Jackie believed that her body would take care of itself.*

Maurice wasn't convinced. He thought it would be a good idea for Jackie to get away to a warmer climate for a week or ten days.

---

*According to Jan Pottker, the author of *Janet & Jackie: The Story of a Mother and Her Daughter, Jacqueline Kennedy Onassis,* after Jackie learned that both her mother and her mother's sister, Win, had Alzheimer's, "she was terrified. Back in New York, she tossed out all her aluminum pans because aluminum cookware had erroneously been linked to the disease."

And he suggested that they sail south on his boat, a seventy-foot, well-appointed yacht named the *Relemar*.* He and Jackie could stop to dine at various ports on their way. She loved being on the boat, away from prying eyes and the pressure of living up to other people's expectations.

But Jackie did not want to leave her grandchildren during the Christmas holiday. Rose, Tatiana, and baby Jack had become her pride and joy. She was also becoming increasingly preoccupied by her son, John. He seemed at loose ends, both personally and professionally. Maurice advised her not to interfere in John's life, and Jackie agreed that it was always unwise for a mother to try to tell her adult son what to do.

"If you play your cards right and give them their freedom," Jackie told the writer Judith Thurman, "they'll stay faithful to you. And when you're a hideous, decrepit old woman, they'll take you to the opera."

But Jackie never followed her own advice when it came to John. Over Maurice's objections, she had prevented John from pursuing a career as an actor, even though that was what he was clearly cut out to be. Instead, she had persuaded him to go to law school, and after he graduated, she urged him to join the district attorney's office in Manhattan. When he quit that job to pursue a different dream—starting his own magazine—Jackie was sorely disappointed.

"I want him to do something meaningful," she said. "Something that will reflect well on the family name."

Maurice tried to explain to Jackie that she was pushing John so hard that he would inevitably push back and rebel. She should not insist that John fit into her preconceived notions of what the son of a slain president should do with his life. Jackie nodded in agree-

---

*The *Relemar* was named after Tempelsman's three children—Rena, Leon, and Marcy.

ment. But she intended to have a heart-to-heart talk with John over the Christmas holiday.

oooooo

When she arrived at her house in Peapack, which she called "my sanctuary away from Manhattan," Jackie found that her caretaker had built a welcoming fire in the fireplace. She sat alone for a while, sorting through the thick Sunday *New York Times*. She was about to throw away the TV section when she spotted a photograph of Daryl Hannah on its glossy cover. Daryl was dressed in a skimpy outfit for the HBO remake of *Attack of the 50 Ft. Woman*.

The subject of Daryl created dissension between mother and son. Jackie did not actively dislike Daryl, but the two women had never really connected.

"Jackie never used one of her favorite words to describe Daryl," said one of Jackie's best friends. "She never said, 'Oh, isn't Daryl great!' Which says a lot about how she felt about her."

On the occasions when John brought Daryl back to the New York apartment for dinner, Jackie usually stayed in her bedroom and ate alone on a tray.

Now, from her living room in Peapack, Jackie picked up the phone and called a friend in New York.

"Have you seen that photo of Daryl in the *Times* TV listings?" she asked. "Gosh, don't you think it makes her look like a giant Amazon cave woman!"

○○○○○○

Daryl wasn't the only topic on which mother and son clashed. Their discussions about his proposed magazine frequently ended with John raising his voice to his mother, storming out of the room, and slamming the door behind him.

The magazine was the brainchild of Michael Berman, John's partner in Random Ventures, who persuaded John to quit his job with the Manhattan district attorney's office.

"There wasn't another person in the world I could have done the magazine with," said Berman. "John brought a whole other dimension to the project. He was a very bright guy, extremely articulate, with an extraordinary vocabulary. He would read several books a week. He read very thoughtful magazines. He had experienced everything in the world. There wasn't a topic he couldn't discuss."*

"John has never shown the slightest interest in magazines before," Jackie told a friend in the publishing business. "And he has no experience in journalism. Why would he want to start this magazine *George*? Especially since it's going to be a magazine that pries into people's private lives. He knows I don't approve of that."

"John loved his mother, and was very close to her, but he was a

---

*The name *George* was the idea of Lou Adler, who produced *The Rocky Horror Picture Show*, and who was married to Daryl Hannah's sister, Page.

pretty explosive guy," said one of Jackie's best friends. "He had a very volatile relationship with his mother during the last few years of her life. She told him that he couldn't be an actor, and she obviously wasn't crazy about his choice of girlfriend, and she sure didn't get his magazine idea for *George*. Jackie wanted him to do something of substance, something worthwhile. She worried about him."

Despite their battles, Jackie was proud of her son. She considered John to be a good person—decent, well-mannered, thoughtful, loyal, and open to new ideas. But John was also very immature: more boy than man. He cruised around the city in a ridiculous backward-turned baseball cap and in-line skates. To Jackie, he often acted like an overgrown frat boy.

Because John was only three years old at the time of his father's assassination, he and Jackie were much closer than most sons and mothers. She feared that one day, when she was no longer around to look after him, something awful would happen to him.

○○○○○○

Shortly after Christmas, Jackie sat down with John for a serious talk. She soon got around to expressing her concern over John's penchant for risky behavior. He attempted every form of extreme sport. He rappelled down the sides of mountains, kayaked alone up the Hudson River—one of the most trafficked waterways in America—and was talking of buying his own airplane.

Jackie had encouraged John to travel and to have new experiences. She once sent him to Micronesia on a deep-sea diving expedition.

"One day Jackie and I were having lunch," recalled one of her friends, "and I said, 'Don't you worry about John riding a bike without a helmet?' And she said, 'No, I don't worry about it at all.'

"She was extremely fatalistic, I think," this friend continued. "I always ascribed it to her European brand of Catholicism.

There's much more of an acceptance of death in Europe than in America. Maybe because of all that she had been through, she had become fatalistic. Everybody other than Jackie would have been concerned about John's risk-taking."

However, there was one activity at which Jackie drew the line: she vehemently disapproved of John's obsession with flying. And now, here in Peapack, she begged him to promise her that he would never fly his own plane. After all, she reminded him, his Kennedy relatives had been dying in plane crashes at the rate of one every seven years for the past fifty years.

"Please don't do it," Jackie said. "There have been too many deaths in the family already. Please promise."

"I promise," John assured his mother.

But John was already secretly signed up to take flying lessons. In order to keep this activity from his mother, he had obtained flight insurance through the Kennedy family business office in Rockefeller Center, rather than through his mother's insurance broker.

His promise not to fly was a falsehood, motivated by the desire of a loving son to set his mother's mind at rest.

A Man with a Hidden Life

*J*ust before New Year's, Jackie and Maurice Tempelsman slipped away on his yacht and sailed to the warm waters of the Caribbean. Although Maurice was an expert sailor and could handle the boat by himself, he took along a captain, a cook, and a butler.

Standing at the helm, Maurice hardly cut a dashing nautical figure. At five foot eight, he was barely an inch taller than Jackie. He had a long, sharp nose and a middle-age spread (he was sixty-three years old) that stretched the waist of his cotton yachting sweater.

Jackie and Maurice struck many people as a curious couple. She was a living legend; he was an obscure diamond merchant. She was athletic, outdoorsy, fun-loving; he was physically unfit. She was a Roman Catholic; he was a Jew. She was born in East Hampton, Long Island, and reared in aristocratic surroundings; he was born in Europe and came from a modest background. She had lost two husbands; he was still married to his first wife.

However, like John Kennedy and Aristotle Onassis before him, Maurice was a man with a clandestine life.

His interest in diamonds and the dangerous places they came from—and the menacing men who controlled them—began back in Europe, where he was born in the Belgian port city of Antwerp, one of the major diamond-cutting centers in the world. As a boy, Maurice had big dreams, and he saw diamonds as his passport out of a drab, middle-class life. In the 1930s, his Yiddish-speaking parents fled the Nazis and came to New York, where Maurice's father became a minor diamond broker.

Maurice joined the firm and took it to new heights of prosperity. In the late 1950s, one of his lawyers, Ted Sorensen, introduced him to Senator John Kennedy, who was then seeking the presidential nomination of the Democratic Party. Kennedy was interested in making contact with Sir Ernest Oppenheimer, the South African magnate who controlled the De Beers diamond cartel, and at his initial meeting with Maurice, the young senator was accompanied by his beautiful wife, Jacqueline.

Maurice was deeply impressed by Jackie, who possessed all the qualities he yearned for in a woman—beauty, brains, sophistication—but found missing in his own wife. Jackie and Maurice hit it off, and when, a few years later, First Lady Jacqueline Kennedy came to New York to attend the opera or a concert with UN ambassador Adlai Stevenson, she frequently asked Maurice to join them.

According to State Department cables, Maurice was an agent of the Oppenheimers in South Africa. He always denied that charge, but his close ties to Larry Devlin, a former CIA station chief in Kinshasa, the capital of Zaire, led to speculation that Maurice was also part of the CIA's operation in the heart of Africa.

By the early 1980s, when Maurice moved into Jackie's apartment, he was a very rich man. He owned three million shares of Lazard Kaplan, his diamond business, and he had interests in a number of other businesses. Altogether, his net worth was estimated by someone familiar with his finances to be about a hundred million dollars.

"Maurice is one of the shrewdest people I've ever met, and one of the best-connected people in the country," said a person who was intimately acquainted with the major players in New York City and Washington, D.C. "He knows everybody in power."

Maurice liked to invite friends and acquaintances to his office, where he held wide-ranging intellectual conversations over lunch. And though he was not an original thinker in the areas of politics and foreign affairs, he had a subtle mind. There was never a misplaced word in what he said. As a result, he was sought after by society hostesses as a dinner guest.

"The very qualities that cause the best people in New York to rave about Maurice now are the qualities that made him valuable to De Beers in Africa," said the *New Yorker* writer Brendan Gill, who was a friend of Jackie's. "The charm, the attractiveness, the many languages, the suavity—all this made him indispensable. When it comes to Maurice's relationship with some of the worst dictators in Black Africa, I think we're treading on the territory of Balzac. I mean, *The Human Condition.* There's a huge novel about good and evil in Maurice's story."

A Touch of the Rogue

*J*ackie had always been attracted to men like Maurice—strong father figures with a touch of the rogue.

The writer Judith Thurman tried to explain the puzzling contradiction between the cautious, prudent, "good" Jackie and the "brazen" Jackie who was attracted to dangerous, decadent men like her father.

"Decadence as an aesthetic," Thurman wrote, ". . . particularly appeals to artistically inclined daughters of privilege, like Jackie, who are raised by prim mothers and neglected by glamorously wild fathers they adore, and who feel that their vital flame has been stifled by the tyranny of convention. Such wasted good girlhoods in white gloves often breed grandiosity . . . along with an insatiable covetousness for experience."

Jackie's first serious romance was with John Phillips Marquand Jr., a son of the famous author who had written such best-selling novels of WASP manners as *The Late George Apley* and *H. M. Pulham, Esquire.* Young Marquand and Jackie met in 1950, during Jackie's junior year abroad in France. He was only a year or two

older than Jackie, but he seemed much more worldly, perhaps because he had seen action during the closing days of World War II.

Like many of the men Jackie was attracted to during her lifetime, Marquand's nickname was Jack. He liked nightlife, and took Jackie to all the hot spots in Paris, including a left-bank hangout that was popular among young Americans and was called L'Elephant Blanc.

Late one night, as they were going up to Marquand's apartment on the old-fashioned, open-grille French elevator, Jackie lost her usual tight self-control. She and Marquand made love in the elevator as it slowly ascended to his floor.

ooooooo

Of course, even before Jack Marquand came along, there had been another Jack in Jackie's life—her father, John Vernou "Black Jack" Bouvier.

Whenever Jackie spent time with her father, he would use the visit as an occasion to coach her on fashion, antiques, and interior decoration. But his favorite subject was the battle of the sexes. From the time Jackie was old enough to understand the difference between men and women, her father engaged her in conversations about sex.

When Jackie was a teenager, her father visited her frequently at boarding school at Miss Porter's in Farmington, Connecticut. Though some people sneered at Miss Porter's as a finishing school, it was actually, for its time, a first-class educational institution that trained women how to act responsibly in the culture in which they were growing up.

Jackie kept a horse at Miss Porter's. It required quite a bit of money to board and care for a horse—money that Jackie's father, who lost his fortune in the depression, did not have. Instead, her grandfather on her mother's side, a pudgy, cigar-chomping real-estate developer by the name of James T. Lee, sent a weekly stipend so that Jackie could keep the horse—and keep up appearances—at the exclusive school.

Thanks to Grandpa Lee, Jackie saddled up her horse every afternoon, regardless of the weather, and galloped off across the rolling Connecticut countryside. The only days on which she did not ride were those on which her father visited. She would wait for her father's arrival in her dormitory room. He was usually late. When he finally pulled up in front of Jackie's dorm in his snazzy convertible, his dark, handsome face beaming in the sunshine, he announced his presence with a special honk of the horn.

Jackie burst out the door, flew into his arms, and kissed him on the lips.

They would stroll arm in arm around the campus. And after a while, they would play a special game. Jackie would point to a mother of one of her classmates.

"That one, Daddy?" she asked.

"Not yet," her father replied, indicating that he had not slept with the woman in question.

Jackie pointed to another and asked: "That one, Daddy?"

"Oh, yes," he said. "I've had her already."

"And that one, Daddy?"

"Yes. That one, too."

Her father's unapologetic libertinism set a pattern for all the men Jackie found attractive in the years to come.

New York, New York

October 1965

(Twenty-nine years earlier)

After she leaves Washington and moves to New York City, Jackie is escorted around town by Sydney Gruson, the short, dapper foreign editor of *The New York Times*.

Sydney bears a striking resemblance to Claude Rains, the Hollywood character actor who starred along with Humphrey Bogart in *Casablanca*. And, in many ways, Sydney is an actor himself. Born in Dublin, Ireland, to a poor Jewish family, he immigrated to Canada and then to the United States as a young man and never attended college. Nonetheless, during his various foreign assignments for the *Times* before he became foreign editor, Sydney managed to acquire a sophisticated wit, a discriminating taste, and a vaguely upper-class British accent.

Some of Jackie's friends are sorely puzzled by her choice of a journalist for a companion. After all, doesn't Jackie hate the press and everything it stands for? But it is really no mystery why Jackie likes Sydney. He is exceedingly charming, fun to be around, and a great storyteller.

What's more, Sydney has an instinctive understanding of power. A key element in his rise up the editorial ladder of the *Times* is his close friendship with Arthur "Punch" Sulzberger, the reserved publisher of the paper. Sydney has made himself an indispensable mentor to Punch in all matters having to do with New York social life.

And Sydney plays the same role with Jackie.

"We used to find out-of-the-way restaurants, where I felt Jackie wouldn't be bothered," Gruson recalls. "But it never worked. One night, we came home from a second-rate restaurant on the West Side of Manhattan, where people had come up to our table and asked her to autograph dollar bills and menus.

"I said, 'Jackie, taking you out is like taking out a monument.'

"And she said, 'Yes, and isn't it fun?'

"Of all the people I've ever met, Jackie was the one who understood power best."

THE GOLDEN GREEK

*T*he man who most resembled Jackie's father in his amoral approach to life was Aristotle Onassis.

Ari, as he was known to his friends, was as charming as he was ugly—a short, barrel-chested man with a great deal of animal vitality. At night, when his yacht, the *Christina,* was docked at Skorpios, he would swim alone around the island without bodyguards— a distance of more than one and a half miles.

Because he struck many people as coarse, even primitive, it came as a great surprise to Jackie that she liked him. He introduced her to Greek mythology, a subject of which she was extremely fond. She was impressed by his kind and thoughtful treatment of Caroline and John; in fact, he spent more time with them than he did with his own children, Alexander and Christina.

When it became obvious that Jackie had fallen under Ari's spell, people sought an explanation.

"Jackie became attracted to Ari for a number of reasons," said her good friend Niki Goulandris, the founder of the Goulandris Natural History Museum in Greece. "After the assassination of

Bobby Kennedy, she told me, 'Niki, I was horrified by two assassinations. I didn't know what to think about the safety of my two
children. I wanted to escape.'

"In Greece, she sought a refuge for her mind," Niki continued.
"Did she succeed in finding that refuge? You can never realize your
dreams completely. But she gained a great deal."

Like Jackie's father, Ari had an endless supply of anecdotes
about his sexual escapades, which Jackie enjoyed listening to.
There was, for instance, the story of his brief affair with Eva Perón.

Then there was Ingeborg Dedichen, the beautiful blond daughter of one of Norway's leading shipowners. And then, of course, there was Maria Callas.

It was Callas who interested Jackie the most. Ari had carried on a love affair with Callas for more than a decade, and like everyone else, Jackie was curious to know all there was to know about her.

"I have always had great admiration for Madame Callas," Ari said. "More than her artistic talent, even more than her success as a great singer, what always impressed me was the story of her early struggles as a poor girl in her teens when she sailed through unusually rough and merciless waters."

For Onassis, the wedding to Jackie was a succès d'estime. He had always wanted to be on the front page of every newspaper in the world. Marrying the former first lady of the United States was like closing the biggest deal of his life.

But the question always remained: Did Onassis love Jackie?

"Love?" asked Captain Costa Anastassiadis, the master of Onassis's yacht, the *Christina,* a floating pleasure palace that cost nearly one million dollars a year to run. "I don't think it was proper love with Jackie. With Callas, it was something different. They had things in common. Both started from zero, spoke Greek— shouted Greek—and had achieved fame. Jackie was a methodical person. On Skorpios, she wrote out a program for her children and had it on my desk early every morning. She wasn't Greek."

But, of course, the marriage didn't last. It began to founder in 1973, after the death of Ari's only son, Alexander, in an airplane crash. Ari began to drink heavily. He complained of insomnia. His crushing personal loss was compounded by devastating reversals in business. He told friends that he believed the gods were punishing him. Like the mythological Icarus, whose wax wings melted when he flew too close to the sun, Ari believed that he had overreached himself by marrying Jackie. He was being punished for his hubris, his overweening pride.

Acapulco, Mexico

New Year's Eve, 1973

(Twenty-one years earlier)

A few months after Alexander Onassis's death, Jackie and Ari fly to Mexico to stay with Loel Guiness, the English banking magnate, and his wife, Gloria. A third guest is Eleanor Lambert, the doyenne of fashion public relations and the inventor of the International Best-Dressed List.

"Ari kept saying he wanted Jackie to have property in Mexico so that she could keep horses," Eleanor recalled in an interview with the author several years before she died. "But Jackie was not mad about the idea.

"On New Year's Eve, we all got together and were sitting after dinner in the Guinesses' salon. There were beautiful fireworks, and we walked out on the terrace overlooking the town. And just as it reached midnight, Ari started to cry. He sobbed and sobbed and sobbed over the loss of his only son.

"And Jackie went over and held him in her arms. And she cried with him.

"That was the only time I had seen them touch each other. They had affection for each other, but no great passion. It was a beautiful moment.

"Gloria, Loel, and I faded away, and left them standing there until they got over it, and came back and joined us."

A Hopeless Case

By 1975, three years after the death of his son, Aristotle Onassis was dying. He suffered from myasthenia gravis and acute gallbladder disease. He was flown to Paris, and after an operation at the American Hospital, he was kept alive by a respirator in room 217 of the Eisenhower wing. At times he was delirious and rambled incoherently.

"I was in Paris with Jackie at the time," said Niki Goulandris. "She visited him in the hospital morning, noon, and night, although her time with him was restricted because he was in the intensive care unit. I remember she wanted to go to Notre Dame Cathedral to pray for him. She knew it was a hopeless case.

"Maybe she shouldn't have left Paris," Niki continued, "but she had two children to look after back in New York, and the situation with Ari was unchanged. In any case, she couldn't have known. As soon as she got to New York, she heard that Ari had died, and she came right back."

THE MIDAS TOUCH

*I*f Jackie was no longer an unfinished woman by 1993, most of the credit had to go to Maurice Tempelsman. He had known Jackie for nearly forty years, through her marriages to both Jack Kennedy and Aristotle Onassis, and he had been Jackie's significant other for twelve years—longer than most people realize.

"This thoughtful, unlikely, Jewish gentleman has put an aura of tranquillity around her," said Samuel Pisar, a Paris-based American lawyer who had occasion to observe Jackie with Kennedy, Onassis, and Tempelsman. "Maurice doesn't show her off like Onassis, who considered Jackie another jewel in his crown. Maurice, the diamond merchant, knows better: he protects her, understands her position, and respects her privacy. He's made it possible for her to enter the third act of her life, the act in which life's conflicts are resolved."

Maurice shared Jackie's interest in the arts. After he moved into her apartment, he occupied one of the guest bedrooms and presided over Jackie's small dinner parties. There was a great deal of speculation among Jackie's friends about the nature of the rela-

tionship between Jackie and Maurice—was it sexual or not? No one knew the answer to that question.

What was known, however, was that Maurice's wife of more than forty years, Lily, lived directly across Central Park on the Upper West Side. Lily was an observant Jew of Polish extraction. She and Maurice had three children—Rena, Leon, and Marcy. Though their relationship foundered early in their marriage, Maurice and Lily agreed to stay together while the children grew up.

"Maurice had had a very uncomfortable existence with his wife," said one of his best friends. "I traveled with them to Israel in 1967, and even back then they weren't getting along. They didn't show any real affection for each other. But they stayed together for the sake of their three children."

Maurice was attracted to well-groomed, well-spoken, well-off women who moved gracefully in the highest levels of society. When it came to winning women, he was not in the same league as John Kennedy or Aristotle Onassis, but according to the testimony of several of his conquests, his old-world charms worked wonders.

There were stories that Lily, a rather dour, religious woman who donated her time to Jewish charities, refused to give Maurice a get—a divorce according to Orthodox Jewish law.

"Actually," said Rabbi Arthur Schneier, "Maurice could have gotten a civil divorce if he wanted to. And if he had chosen to marry out of his faith, he wouldn't have needed any kind of permission from his former wife."

The fact of the matter was that Maurice and Jackie were perfectly content with their present arrangement. Neither of them wanted to get married again. Nor did it seem to bother anyone else that Jackie and Maurice were living together without the benefit of a marriage license.

"[I]t was rare to hear or read a word of opprobrium about Tempelsman and [Jackie's] relationship, even from New York's cattier columnists and insatiable tabloids, which never tired of running her photograph," Paula Span wrote in *The Washington Post*. "It was almost as though the press and public had decided she was entitled to grow old with someone. His acceptance by her family probably helped quiet criticism."

oooooo

Maurice was a highly astute financier, and even before he moved in with Jackie, she turned over all her financial affairs to him. He took the inheritance that she received from Onassis—about nineteen million dollars after taxes—and made brilliant use of the money.

During the decade of the 1980s, when the Dow-Jones industrial average quintupled in value, Jackie's investments rose between eight- and tenfold. This meant her original nineteen-million-dollar

inheritance from Onassis grew to about one hundred fifty million dollars.

In addition to her estate in Peapack and her fifteen-room Manhattan co-op, Jackie also owned 464 acres on Martha's Vineyard. The property made up one third of the entire town of Gay Head. Her combined real estate was worth thirty-five million to forty million dollars.

Thus, Jackie's fortune was now very close to two hundred million dollars.

"People have this mania of interest about Jackie and money," said one of her friends. "But her real concern has not been for herself: it's always been for her family, for Caroline and John. The money evens out their place in the Kennedy family. They're not the poor relations."

The Pluses and Minuses of Fame

---

*J*ackie and Maurice hosted intimate dinner parties for ten or twelve people in her apartment and occasionally accepted invitations to other people's homes. One such invitation came in the early 1990s from New York's former mayor Ed Koch, who put together highly programmed dinners at which his guests were asked to discuss a particular subject.

"I did this," he explained, "because women tended not to talk. Horrible as it might seem, they let their husbands or their dates carry the conversation. I always found that upsetting, so I introduced something that women, as well as men, felt comfortable talking about."

Koch always sat in the middle of the table, and at a certain point, he would say, "We have a little practice here to say something about ourselves. I think this creates a focus."

The night Jackie attended, she was seated at the opposite end of the head of the table, and when it came her turn, she started by saying, "My name is Jacqueline Kennedy Onassis, and I am an editor." She then proceeded to tell everyone about her job.

"Everybody loved it," Koch recalled. "She was so understated. And at the end of the evening, she came up to me and said, 'I've never had such a good time.'

"I believe she had such a good time because she was treated like everyone else, and that is what she always wanted."

○○○○○○

Once or twice a week, a yoga teacher named Tillie Weitzner came to Jackie's apartment, and for the next hour Jackie was incommunicado.

"I know Marta [Sgubin], Jackie's Italian maid, who's been with her forever," said a woman friend of twenty years, who asked the author not use her name. "And Marta will always get her to the phone for me. But not when Jackie meditates and does yoga. She stays home a lot more than she used to. When she's home alone with Maurice, they eat early, at seven-thirty. They don't sit around with cocktails and TV. They get on with things. And they go to bed early."

Jackie's public forays were few and far between. She carefully picked her causes. She chaired the annual fund-raising gala for the American Ballet Theatre, and she joined several dignified protests against objectionable skyscrapers.

For example, Jackie helped the Municipal Art Society save Grand Central Station, Lever House, and St. Bartholomew's Church. In this effort, she was assisted by Brendan Gill, who in addition to writing for *The New Yorker* was president of the Municipal Art Society.

"What Jackie and I would do at almost all of our benefits," Gill recalled for the author, "we would be in the reception line, because she was our star, and I was the old cannon they rolled out for that purpose. And, of course, the reception line was always entertaining to me from a novelistic point of view, because it gave me the chance to watch all the people getting ready to come up there just to shake hands with Jackie. And she was very good at passing people along.

"I would have to say, over and over, 'Mrs. Onassis, this is so-and-so,' about somebody who had been waiting an hour in line, and for whom there was no need for identification. But that was the protocol. And she could really pass them on. Again, I think this is the White House training. The Trumps and people like that would come, and she would get them through in no time flat.

"We had an entertaining time at those fund-raisers, in part because Jackie had a perfectly lively sense of the degree to which she was being used, and the purpose to which she was prepared to consent to be made use of. And I think that's a highly credible thing for her to have done."

oooooo

Jackie's attitude toward the media was shaped by still-raw memories of two Kennedy assassinations and the tabloid onslaught caused by her marriage to Onassis. Wherever she went, she detonated a media explosion.

"A few years ago," recalled the art critic John Richardson, "I was Jackie's escort for a rather dazzling gala at the Metropolitan Opera. There were masses of photographers, and she said to me, 'Look, there's going to be a mob scene, and I asked my driver to meet us downstairs.' But her car wasn't there. We were kept waiting for ten minutes, absolutely surrounded by the press, and they were popping on and on with their cameras, and it was terrifying, blinding, and she was completely unnerved."

Though she seemed to be surrounded by reporters and photographers all the time, Jackie rarely met one-on-one with a working journalist. She once made an exception and consented to talk to a woman writer for *The New Yorker,* who was doing a profile on one of Jackie's favorite Doubleday authors, John Loring, the design director of Tiffany & Co.

"Yes," Jackie told Loring, "I will talk to this *New Yorker* woman, which is not what I do. And I'm going to have a lot of Kennedys very annoyed with me by doing this, because they have frequently asked for my support in the press, and I always tell them that I don't break my rule speaking to the press about anything. But I think it would be unfair to you who have spent so much time and so many years working with me, and then someone does this profile in *The New Yorker,* and I am not there at all, as though all those years never happened, and we never did all that wonderful work together."

However, when Jackie sat down with *The New Yorker* writer, she immediately sensed danger. The woman seemed a bit too interested in Jackie's private life. And so, Jackie simply got up from her chair and walked out of the interview.

She then called Loring and said, "You're going to be very, very annoyed with me and very disappointed, but I cannot do that interview. And in any case, you don't really want me in that profile, because people will only remember me, and you'll just be forgotten completely if I'm in that piece."

○ ○ ○ ○ ○ ○

This was not the first time—nor the last—that Jackie acknowledged her power over others. When people played hard to get for books she was working on, Jackie said, "Oh, if I have to go and beat them up, I will. Because with their social pretensions, they wouldn't dare say no to me."

She despised café society and self-promoters.

"Those people," she said, "really get my back up."

But she could be extremely generous, too. There was, for instance, the case of a Japanese woman who worked at Tiffany & Co. and wanted to buy a cooperative apartment in a good building on the Upper East Side. She called John Loring and said, "I found an apartment that I really love, but you can guess how it's going to be, because I'm Japanese. They're not going to let me into this building. And I really want the apartment. And, you know, I've worked with you and Mrs. Onassis on various book projects, and I wonder, do you suppose she would write a note for me, because if she does, the board of the building will probably let me in."

Loring called Jackie to ask if she would consider writing such a note.

"Jackie cut me short when she heard the name of the apartment building," Loring recalled. "Jackie said, 'You don't need to say another word. The letter will be on your desk in thirty minutes.'

"And thirty minutes later, the letter was there and the woman got her apartment."

ooooo

But Jackie was also painfully aware of the obstacles that fame placed in her path.

"Jackie would frequently say that she'd like to go on a photo shoot to some exotic place like Beijing," Loring recalled. "'Well,' I'd say, 'Jackie, come along.' And she'd say, 'I want to go there, I want to see Beijing, can I come along? That would be so great.' And I'd say, 'Well, why don't you just do it? You know it could be arranged.' And then, her face would cloud over and she would get that worried look, and she'd just sigh and say, 'No, the security would be too much. It's just beyond coping with. It's impossible, it's impossible.' And so there was all that in her life: there were so many things that were impossible."

Some of Jackie's friends believed that she did not want to avoid publicity as much as she wanted to control it. Like other great public personalities, she had a connoisseur's appreciation of her own stardom, and the power that it conveyed.

"It Can't Possibly Be Jackie O!"

As someone who lunched with Jackie and frequently chatted on the phone with her, I always thought of her as an encyclopedia of details.

She was certainly not given to the big thought. She did not warm up to subjects like "What Is Life?" "What Is Art?" "What Does It All Mean?" She did not like conversations that went round and round in intellectual circles, where there was no place for her to jump on and off.

That was not the Jackie I knew for a dozen years before her death.

In order to maintain her sanity, she focused totally on the details of what was going on at the moment. Her mind never wandered off. She enjoyed the nitty-gritty of daily living. In this respect, she struck me as being very French, because she was in tune with the French attitude that life is made up of small details.

Her references to John Kennedy and Aristotle Onassis were curiously alike. When she spoke of them, she used the same tone

of voice, and she conveyed the feeling that she had learned a great deal from Kennedy and Onassis and still admired their way of life.

Though it was many years since Kennedy and Onassis had died, Jackie left the rather bizarre impression that she still deferred to their opinions. It was, "Ari said this, Ari didn't like that . . . let's do it the way Ari would have done it." Or it was, "This is the way Jack would have done it in this situation."

In her conversations with friends, she referred to both men on a regular basis. It was not as if a lightbulb would go off above her head occasionally and she would suddenly remember that she was once married to Jack Kennedy and Ari Onassis. No, not at all. At the appropriate moment, she always seemed to have an appropriate thought about these two men, and what they had stood for.

○○○○○○

"In all those years of working with her on those beautifully illustrated Tiffany books," said John Loring, "I never heard Jackie once say, 'Oh, isn't that silver tureen beautiful?' Or, 'Isn't that a great painting?' Or, 'Aren't those chairs nice?' She had no particular interest in objects per se.

"But, she would say, 'Oh, look what they did with that.' It was never, 'Look at that.' It was, 'Isn't it wonderful what they did with that.' It was how people put it together, what they put on it, how they presented the thing. It was always, 'She does the greatest things with something.' The inanimate object held no interest for Jackie whatsoever.

"It was the people and what they did, their personal style. When, for instance, she said Jack liked this or Ari liked that, it was never a thing she was talking about. It was their behavior.

"I brought back four simple cups from a trip to Nepal that cost ten dollars each in a street market, and Jackie said, 'Oh, I'd just give up iced tea and drink watermelon squash all summer long if I had those cups.' So that afternoon, I went home and wrapped them up and put them in a cardboard box, and the next morning I sent them by messenger to Doubleday. And she called me and said, 'You created quite a stir here. Security thought the package contained a canister bomb, and that someone was trying to blow me up.'"

○○○○○○

When she returned to New York to live full-time after Onassis died in 1975, Jackie was forty-six years old. She seemed deeply troubled, as though she was pursued by invisible demons. She would not talk about what was bothering her, but it was clear to her friends that she was unhappy almost all of the time.

Within a few years, however, she started coming out of her shell

© 1971 Ron Galella

and began enjoying life. Her haunted look disappeared. She was delighted by the way her children were turning out. She was proud of them and exhilarated when she was with them. Anything that had to do with her Caroline and John made her deliriously happy.

The changes that came over her astonished her friends. She no longer wanted to hide in her Doubleday office and eat lunch there all the time. She put on a beautiful silk blouse, thin alligator belt, dark slacks, and went out to eat.

And she no longer hid from the public. She stood on line, like everybody else, to buy tickets to a movie. She did not travel behind dark-tinted glass in a chauffeur-driven limousine. She was often seen walking down Fifth Avenue in the middle of the afternoon, prompting looks of astonishment from passersby. She seemed to get a kick out of seeing people stare at her and say to each other, "No, it can't be, it can't possibly be Jackie O!"

○○○○○○

And so, by the winter of 1994, her life had reached a kind of plateau of contentment. However, early in January, while sailing in the Caribbean with Maurice, the deep, hacking cough, which had been dogging Jackie ever since her hunting accident, returned. Except now it was worse than ever.

She asked a local doctor to prescribe antibiotics. But the drug did not work, and she soon developed painful swelling in the lymph nodes in her neck. What was even more alarming, she began to feel stabbing pains in her stomach.

At the urging of Maurice, Jackie telephoned her New York internist, who treated many famous patients. The doctor asked Jackie to describe her symptoms. When she was finished, he ordered Jackie to get on the next available plane and fly back home.

Jackie protested that she was on vacation. She could see a doctor after she and Maurice sailed back to New York later in the month.

But her doctor insisted.

There was no time to lose.

Otis Air Force Base Hospital and
Boston Children's Hospital, Massachusetts
August 7–9, 1963
(Thirty years earlier)

"That's it," President John Fitzgerald Kennedy says. "There's no time to lose. We're going to Otis."

He has just been informed by Dr. Janet Travell, his personal physician, that his wife has gone into premature labor and is about to undergo a cesarean section at Otis Air Force Base Hospital. The president's Air Force aide, Godfrey McHugh, has a plane standing by.

The flight from Washington takes just thirty minutes, but by the time the president touches down, the baby is already born. He weighs four pounds, one ounce. He is so sickly that a Catholic chaplain is summoned to come and baptize him while he lies in a pressurized incubator. He is named Patrick Bouvier Kennedy.

One of Jack's oldest friends, Larry Newman, is waiting for him in the hospital.

"He came over and made a move as if he were going to put his arm around my shoulder," Newman recalls, "then just shook hands and said, 'Thanks for being here. It made me feel so much better knowing you were here.'

"I've never seen him more emotional," Newman continues. "The way he said it, I was very close to tears. And I don't cry very easily."

Later, Evelyn Lincoln, the president's personal secretary, finds him sitting on a bed in a hospital room. He is staring into space.

"How are things with little Patrick?" Evelyn asks.

"He has a fifty-fifty chance," the president replies.

"That's all a Kennedy needs," says Evelyn. "He will make it."

But the tiny boy is suffering from hyaline membrane disease, a respiratory disease in prematurely born infants. He is flown to Children's Hospital in Boston.

The president commutes by helicopter between Otis, where Jackie is recuperating, and Children's Hospital, where he dons a white surgical gown and cap and watches as his son fights for his life.

At three o'clock in the morning on August 9, a Secret Service man comes into the room where the president and his close aide, Dave Powers, are catching some sleep.

"Dave," the Secret Service man says, "the doctor has told me the baby has taken a turn for the worse."

Dave wakes Jack, and they go to Patrick's side.

"I was with him at the hospital when he was holding Patrick's hand and the nurse said, 'He's gone,'" Evelyn says, "and tears came into his eyes. I had never seen tears in his eyes before."

"He just cried and cried and cried and cried," Dave says.

Patrick has lived fewer than thirty-nine hours, and all Jack can say when it is over is, "It is against the laws of nature for parents to bury their children."

Jackie is devastated when Jack breaks the news to her. But she tells him that they will somehow manage to go on with their lives.

"The one blow I could not bear," Jackie tells Jack, "would be to lose you."

III

The Onus of the Disease

January 1994

PRAYING FOR A SIGN FROM GOD

On Monday, January 10—seven weeks since her fall—Jackie walked into the office of Dr. Carolyn Agresti, a head and neck surgeon at New York Hospital–Cornell Medical Center. The doctor had dealt with famous patients before, but none of the magnitude of Jackie. Being only human, she was impressed—both with Jackie and with herself for being chosen as Jackie's physician—and she did not want to unduly alarm Jackie when she found enlarged lymph nodes in her neck and armpit.

Swollen lymph nodes could mean any number of things, Dr. Agresti explained, including that Jackie had a low-grade infection. To be on the safe side, she suggested that Jackie have a CAT scan.

Jackie had had CAT scans before, and she did not see any reason to tell Maurice Tempelsman or her children about Dr. Agresti's initial findings. For one thing, the doctor did not seem particularly alarmed. For another, as the child of an alcoholic father and a temperamental mother, Jackie had developed a well-honed talent for denial. As she herself once put it, "I simply ignore the unpleasant."

However, a few days later on her next visit, Dr. Agresti informed Jackie that the CAT scan revealed that there were swollen lymph nodes in other parts of her body as well—both in her chest and in a place deep in her abdomen known as the retroperitoneal area. This time, the doctor said, they needed to get a biopsy of the lymph nodes.

And yet, even as the warning signs grew more serious, Jackie continued to keep her condition a secret. It was as though she believed she would only make matters worse by putting it into words.

On her third visit, which took place toward the end of January, Jackie sat across the desk from Dr. Agresti, who appeared to be struggling to keep a neutral expression on her face. But there was no way for the doctor to soften the blow. The biopsy, she informed Jackie, confirmed that she had non-Hodgkin's lymphoma.

Jackie looked as though she had not heard.

"I'm sorry," the doctor repeated, "you have non-Hodgkin's lymphoma."

"I can't believe it," Jackie managed to say when she had recovered from her shock. "I've always taken such good care of myself. I've followed all the rules of healthy living. Except for smoking."

The doctor offered a few words of comfort.

Jackie did not display any self-pity. She did not break down, or cry, or ask, "Why me?" She was very poised and dignified.

"Jackie has a truly aristocratic nature," explained her friend, the novelist Gita Mehta. "And the essence of that nature is a sense of responsibility. Her first thought is never for herself. It is always for others, especially her children."

After Jackie left the doctor's office, she would go directly to the Church of St. Thomas More on East Eighty-ninth Street, between Madison and Park Avenues. It was the week after Epiphany, the Christian feast commemorating the first manifestation of Christ to the Gentiles.

As soon as she knelt, she began crying. Between sobs, she prayed for a sign from God.

○○○○○○

Jackie found solace in her spiritual life as a Roman Catholic.

Her mother, Janet Auchincloss, had been excommunicated by the Catholic Church for marrying Auchincloss. For the rest of her life, whenever Janet was around high-ranking Church officials, she betrayed her feelings of guilt as a lapsed Catholic by being unusually obsequious.

Before Janet was excommunicated, she sent Jackie for religious instruction to a convent run by the Society of the Helpers of the Holy Souls, a religious order of Catholic women founded in Paris in 1856. The nuns' headquarters were on Manhattan's Upper East

Side, and they were accustomed to educating the daughters of the rich.

The French nuns taught Jackie how to sew, administer first aid, visit and care for the poor, and "pray, suffer, and labor for the souls in purgatory." They demanded that Jackie sit up straight and memorize the catechism. The slightest infraction of the nuns' rules earned Jackie a hard crack across the back of her neck or wrist with a long wooden pointer.

The nuns' cruelty left Jackie with ambivalent feelings about a church that allowed such treatment of children and other defenseless human beings. And these feelings intensified when the Vatican threatened to excommunicate her in 1968 after she announced her intention to marry Aristotle Onassis, a member of the Greek Orthodox Church. Ever since, Jackie had cultivated her own version of Catholicism.

She was unmoved by conventional displays of piety, such as the proper way to pray the rosary (though she never forgot what the nuns had taught her: "One, make the sign of the cross and say the Apostles' Creed; two, say the Our Father; three, say three Hail Marys . . ."). Jackie was stimulated by the aesthetic and spiritual qualities of the Church: its great cathedrals, religious paintings, and statues, its sublime music, and the compelling mystery of the mass. She believed that Beauty, Love, and Mercy led to salvation.

She found special comfort in the Catholic belief in the resurrection of the body, when those people whose sins were forgiven by God would be reunited with their loved ones for eternity.

"After I die," she told a priest, "I fully expect to meet Jack [Kennedy] in heaven."

○○○○○○

The first person she told about her diagnosis was Maurice.

When he came home that evening, the apartment was curiously quiet. Jackie usually played music when she was home alone, but the only sound Maurice heard was the dim, ever-present hum of city buses fifteen floors below on Fifth Avenue.

He found Jackie alone in the living room, standing in front of one of the tall French windows, which was covered in gray draperies that pooled on the polished, dark-wood floor. The draperies had been made by a famous designer named John Palor, who also decorated the library.

From time to time, Jackie asked the well-known interior decorator Mark Hampton to "fluff up" the slipcovers and the rugs, but he always left the apartment looking old, because that was the way Jackie liked it. The living room had not been painted in a long time (parts of the ceiling were cracked and peeling), and the draperies were twenty-five years old. Yet nothing looked shabby or out of style.

Jackie and Maurice moved into the library. Here there were towering bookshelves, large tables covered with books and papers, and comfortable sofas. One volume stood out from all the rest: a huge red leather-bound book that Jackie had put together as a present for Aristotle Onassis. In her own handwriting, Jackie had filled the book with English translations from Homer's *Odyssey.* Then she had pasted in photographs that she had taken of Onassis, comparing him with Odysseus.

Maurice could tell by the expression on Jackie's face that something was wrong. However, nothing could have prepared him for what Jackie told him.

"I have cancer," she said.

HIGH MAINTENANCE

$\mathcal{I}$ refuse to believe that I am going to die," Jackie said.

Caroline and John were sitting on a sofa on either side of their mother, hugging her, and crying as they had not cried since they were children. A few feet away, Maurice watched the scene, his eyes brimming with tears.

There were a hundred questions to be asked and answered.

When did you hear?

What did the doctor say?

What do you have to do?

What's the prognosis? . . .

Jackie tried to assure them that her type of cancer, non-Hodgkin's lymphoma, was not a death sentence.

"People hear the word *cancer*," she said, "and they immediately assume that it's fatal. But they're wrong. Doctors have made huge strides treating cancer. Believe me, I'm going to beat this. I'll survive. Won't I, Maurice?"

"Of course you will," Maurice said. "You're going to live to see

John marry and have children, and you're going to be around when his kids graduate from college."

John made an attempt to laugh through his tears.

In fact, John was further away from marriage than ever. Unbeknownst to Jackie, he was no longer seeing Daryl Hannah exclusively. He had recently met and fallen in love with a stunning, six-foot-tall blond named Carolyn Bessette, who worked in the public relations department of Calvin Klein. They had just begun dating.

John suspected that Carolyn Bessette would not be his mother's cup of tea, any more than Daryl Hannah had been. Carolyn shared none of his mother's cultural interests—in literature, ballet, or the arts. Carolyn was strictly a downtown girl, who was into fashion and style. She did recreational drugs, and gave off exciting vibes—edgy and dangerous.

John knew Carolyn would be high maintenance, but he did

not care. He had intended to introduce his mother to Carolyn after they had been dating for a little while longer. Now that his mother had cancer, however, he decided to postpone the meeting.

Caroline Kennedy Schlossberg seemed to be even more broken up than her brother. She had been six years old when her father was assassinated and, unlike her brother, who had been only three, she remembered everything about that day.

Caroline not only looked like the Kennedy side of the family, she had the Kennedys' fatalistic Irish take on life. But her tough exterior hid a vulnerable core, and she found the prospect of losing another parent unbearable.

She clung to her mother and could not stop crying.

"I want you to promise me one thing," Caroline said between sobs.

"What's that?" Jackie asked.

"That you'll stop smoking."

Like all heavy smokers, Jackie knew that she had been playing Russian roulette with her life.

"You have to stop smoking," Caroline insisted, "if only for the sake of Rose, Tatiana, and Jack. They need you."

At the mention of the names of her grandchildren, Jackie was filled with guilt.

"Yes, I'll stop smoking," Jackie promised.

Then she began to weep, too. Not for herself, but for her grandchildren. They were so young. Jackie could recall when her own children were about the same age as Rose and Tatiana, and how they reacted to a death in the family.

Washington, D.C.
January 15, 1964
(Thirty years earlier)

About two months after the assassination, Jackie moves into a town house in Georgetown and takes up residence as a kind of living monument to her martyred husband. When tour buses go by the house, Jackie can hear the voice of the guide over the loudspeaker.

". . . And this is the home of Jackie Kennedy, Caroline, and John-John. . . ."

Jackie a wreck. She can hardly function. From time to time, she allows visits by Jack Kennedy's former associates, including Defense Secretary Robert McNamara.

"I was a little bit in love with her," McNamara confesses years later. "Everybody was."

McNamara has brought a present, an unfinished oil portrait of the president. The painter has completed Kennedy's face and shoulders but has left a large part of the canvas bare. The artist came to McNamara and said that he had been working on the portrait from life and that he had a few more sittings to go when the president died.

"I bought it," McNamara tells Jackie, "and if you want it, it's yours."

Jackie is extremely fond of Bob McNamara. He played a key role in helping her pick out Jack Kennedy's grave site in Arlington National Cemetery, a spot just below the Curtis-Lee Mansion that is in a direct line of sight with the Lincoln Memorial and the Washington Monument.

Now, gazing at the oil portrait McNamara has given her, Jackie is once again deeply touched by his thoughtfulness.

"Oh, Bob," she says, "it's lovely. Such a good likeness. It captures Jack. I'm going to hang it in a prominent place."

However, a few days later, when Jackie phones McNamara, her voice betrays her distress.

"Bob," she says, "I'm so sorry, but I can't keep your wonderful gift. You must take the portrait back."

"For heaven's sake, why?" he asks.

"It's not that I don't like it," she says. "I do. But I had it on the floor in the dining room, leaning against the wall where I was going to hang it. And Caroline and John came in and saw it. And they starting kissing it. . . . Oh, Bob, it's simply more than I can stand."

A KIND OF HUBRIS

$\mathcal{M}$aurice was a man of action, and he immediately set out to make certain that Jackie was receiving the best care modern medicine could provide.

His initial inquiries of Jackie's doctors were not as encouraging as Jackie had led him to believe. To begin with, he learned that doctors divided lymphomas, or cancerous tumors of the lymph system, into two types: Hodgkin's disease (named for Thomas Hodgkin, a nineteenth-century London physician who distinguished the cancer from tuberculosis) and a dozen other forms grouped as non-Hodgkin's lymphomas.

In addition, Jackie had an aggressive form of the cancer. The cells were anaplastic—that is, they were undeveloped, what doctors called embryonic or primitive, indicating that the disease was highly malignant and could spread to other parts of Jackie's body.

The doctors informed Maurice that people with non-Hodgkin's had a median survival rate of only seven and a half years, and in more than half the cases, it proved incurable. Of the forty-five thousand non-Hodgkin's lymphoma cases that would be diagnosed this year in the United States, nearly twenty-three thousand of the patients were expected to die from the disease.

Thus, Jackie's chances of survival were fifty-fifty, at best.

Beyond the question of Jackie's long-term chances of survival, there was also the more immediate question of her mental outlook. Maurice had friends with cancer, and he knew that the disease was often accompanied by feelings of shame.

And so Maurice began learning everything he could about cancer. He read many books, including one of the best, *Illness as Metaphor,* the landmark essay written by Susan Sontag when she was a cancer patient herself.

"Cancer patients are lied to," Sontag wrote, "not just because the disease is (or is thought to be) a death sentence, but because it is felt to be obscene—in the original meaning of that word: ill-omened, abominable, repugnant to the senses. . . .

"According to the mythology of cancer, it is generally a steady repression of feeling that causes the disease. In the earlier, more optimistic form of this fantasy, the repressed feelings were sexual; now, in a notable shift, the repression of violent feelings is imagined to cause cancer [and the] passion that people think will give them cancer if they don't discharge it is rage. . . . [T]he onus of the disease [is] on the patient."

To make her point, Sontag quoted from W. H. Auden's poem "Miss Gee":

Doctor Thomas sat over his dinner,
    Though his wife was waiting to ring,
Rolling his bread into pellets;
    Said, "Cancer's a funny thing.

"Nobody knows what the cause is
    Though some pretend they do;

It's like some hidden assassin
>   Waiting to strike at you.

"Childless women get it,
>   And men when they retire;
It's as if there had to be some outlet
>   For their foiled creative fire."

As Maurice knew, Jackie was particularly susceptible to self-blame. She had shared with him her feelings of deep remorse over her behavior as a wife to John Kennedy.

"I was melancholy after the death of our baby [Patrick] and I stayed away . . . longer than I needed to," she said. "And then when I came back [Jack] was trying to get me out of my grief and maybe I was a bit snappish; but I could have made his life so much happier, especially for the last few weeks. I could have tried harder to get over my melancholy."

She even blamed herself for not having done more to save her husband from the assassin's bullets.

"I would have been able to pull him down, or thrown myself in front of him, or do something, if I had only known."

Maurice feared that Jackie would come to regard herself, in Susan Sontag's words, "as one of life's losers."

○○○○○○

"She said, 'I feel it is a kind of hubris,'" Arthur Schlesinger recalled of his conversation with Jackie. "'I have always been proud of keeping fit. I swim, and I jog, and I do my push-ups, and walk around the Reservoir—and now this suddenly happens.'

"She was laughing when she said it," Schlesinger continued. "She seemed cheery and hopeful, perhaps to keep up the spirits of her friends, and her own. Chemotherapy, she added, was not too bad; she could read a book while it was administered. The doctors said that in fifty percent of the cases lymphoma could be stabilized. Maybe she knew it was fatal. Maybe she didn't know at all, but even if she did, she still had hope for some other future."

Jackie's hope was tempered by the tragedies that still haunted her memory. She had suffered the loss of three children—a stillbirth, a miscarriage, and her two-day-old son Patrick Bouvier; two husbands—John F. Kennedy and Aristotle Onassis; a stepson—Alexander Onassis; and a brother-in-law—Robert Kennedy.

She once asked a priest to explain her husband's assassination. "Why, why? How could God do something like that?"

The priest did not have a satisfactory answer then.

And no one had one now.

A ROUTINE MANICURE

*O*nce a week, usually about six P.M., the doorman of 1040 Fifth Avenue buzzed Jackie's apartment to announce the arrival of Natalia Aldea.

A few moments later, the elevator door swung open, and a short woman with a broad Slavic face stepped directly into Jackie's small foyer. A black-and-white marble floor led her into a long, wide gallery that contained a console and antique gilt mirror flanked by tall Chinese porcelain vases filled with branches.

Marta escorted Natalia into the library, where the walls were papered in red. And there, beside a big desk, Natalia set up the equipment and soapy water for Jackie's weekly manicure and pedicure.

"I first met Mrs. Onassis when I worked in Kenneth's salon, when he still had that beautiful town house on Fifty-fourth Street," Natalia said. "I used to go to her apartment whenever she called me. She came into the library dressed in the same clothes she had on at work—slacks, very casual. And while I worked on her, she would be on the phone, talking to people, sometimes writing things down.

"She liked to keep her nails and toenails natural and clean-looking. She had long fingers, and very beautiful hands. But when she worked hard, and was nervous, she used to bite her nails.

"I heard she was sick. People used to talk about it around the apartment. Marta told me that Mrs. Onassis wasn't well. But I didn't know so many details. I couldn't tell from her fingernails or toenails that anything was wrong with her. And she used to wear some makeup, so I couldn't see real skin.

"I began to hear that she was in and out of the hospital. I noticed that she was beginning to lose her hair. You could tell that she knew exactly what the problem was, and she didn't want anybody coming into her house and seeing her the way she was becoming.

"I did Mrs. Onassis for several weeks after she fell ill. She thought she would become better, but she didn't. And after that, she decided that there was no point in having her hair done, or having a manicure or pedicure. She stopped caring."

But, of course, that was not true. Jackie cared deeply about her personal grooming. Because she was a highly visual person, appearances were extremely important to her. But week by week, the cancer was taking its toll, physically transforming her into a person she did not recognize in the mirror. She was horrified to realize that something as trivial but routine as a manicure was no longer necessary.

It was not that Jackie stopped caring.

She cared too much.

Lenox Hill Hospital, New York
Fall 1985
(Nine years earlier)

Though her colleagues at Doubleday make a valiant effort to treat Jackie as just another acquiring editor—"one of the boys," as it were—the truth is they are deeply in awe of her. Their feelings show in all sorts of strange ways. They lower their voices when they speak to her; whether they are in a good mood or not, they smile when they pass her in the hallway; and they never, ever interrupt her when she is on the phone.

Except this day is different.

One of the company operators cuts into a phone conversation Jackie is having with a Hollywood celebrity. She apologizes profusely, then informs Jackie that Maurice Tempelsman's doctor is holding on the other line.

"Yes, Doctor, what is it?" Jackie asks.

"I've just admitted Maurice to the coronary care unit of Lenox Hill Hospital," the doctor says. "He's complaining of chest pains."

Jackie immediately drops everything and heads straight for the coronary care unit of Lenox Hill Hospital. There, she is informed by Maurice's doctor that he has suffered a mild heart attack. She is devastated. She should have known something like this was going to happen. It's all her fault. She has been trying to get Maurice to do something about his weight and lack of exercise, but she hasn't tried hard enough.

"What can be done?" she asks the doctor.

"Three of Maurice's coronary arteries are clogged," the doctor tells her. "There are only two choices: open-heart surgery or a PTCA."

"A PTCA? What is that?"

"A percutaneous transluminal coronary angioplasty," the doctor explains. "Otherwise known as balloon angioplasty. The goal is to open the artery with a tiny balloon at the end of the catheter by squashing the plaque against the artery's wall."

"Is it safe?" Jackie asks.

"It's a lot safer than open-heart surgery," the doctor replies.

Jackie raises no objections to the procedure, and the doctor goes ahead.

"She moved into the hospital to be with him," says one of Maurice's oldest friends. "I was there, and saw how she behaved. She was very much in love with Maurice. And he with her. You could tell by the way they talked to each other, and looked at each other, and deferred to each other. In all respects, you could see the love. It really was a great love affair. They were two mature people with a lot of experience, and they felt lucky they had found each other."

During an emotional moment in the hospital, when Jackie fears that Maurice is going to die, she impulsively raises the subject of marriage. Neither of them has ever felt the need to change the status of their relationship, but suddenly marriage sounds like a good idea.

Maurice tells Jackie he will get a divorce. He calls his secretary and sends her to buy a gold eternity ring encrusted with emeralds and sapphires. Early the next day, before his operation, he presents the ring to Jackie. There is an inscription inside in French. It is addressed to "Jacks," the nickname Black Jack Bouvier gave Jackie as a child.

As Maurice is wheeled into the operating room, Jackie holds his hand. She is wearing his ring along with the wedding band given to her by Jack Kennedy. If Maurice survives, Jackie intends to become Mrs. Maurice Tempelsman.

But although Maurice pulls through, it doesn't work out that way.

"There were simply too many things in the way of their getting married," says one of Maurice's friends. "The children were not a problem. His kids and hers saw each other and liked each other. But they had different religions. And a legal bond would have made things very complicated financially for both of them, and for their heirs. What's more—and this point cannot be stressed too strongly—Jackie had come to like her independence. She was no longer the woman she had been before. She decided after Maurice got out of the hospital that she did not need or want to be married. She was happy the way things were. Why change it?"

IV

The Shock of Recognition

February 1994

A Cloak-and-Dagger Operation

On February 11, *The New York Times* ran a front-page story revealing that Jackie had been undergoing chemotherapy for about a month.

"She is undergoing a course of treatment and there is every expectation that it will be successful," Nancy Tuckerman, Jackie's childhood friend, confidante, and spokeswoman, said in an interview with the paper. To which the *Times* added this postscript: "Mrs. Onassis decided to disclose the diagnosis of lymphoma because there had been speculation and rumors about her health recently."

Over the course of thirty years, there had always been speculation about Jackie. First, people talked about her as the dewy queen of Camelot. Then, for a while, she was seen as the saintly widow of the martyred president. Following that, she was portrayed as the gold-digging Jackie who married Daddy O (Onassis) and became Jackie O. More recently, she had been the single working mother.

However, the moment the news of Jackie's cancer was flashed around the world, the question of her identity was settled once and for all. The media verdict was unanimous: Jackie's days as the jet-setting, shopaholic wife of the froglike Onassis were forgiven and forgotten. Whatever her past faults, the world once again embraced her uncritically.

"Jackie Kennedy Onassis," Norman Mailer was quoted as saying, "is not merely a celebrity, but a legend; not a legend, but a myth—no, more than a myth: she is now a historic archetype, virtually a demiurge."

Typical of the worldwide coverage was this tribute to Jackie that appeared in *The Baltimore Sun:*

"Although she is a woman whose entire life has been telegraphed through headlines—many of them shocking and tragic—the news that Jacqueline Kennedy Onassis is undergoing chemotherapy for non-Hodgkin's lymphoma shocked and saddened me. . . . Every generation has its defining public figures, the people who tell us who we are. In the last 35 years there have been the obvious ones— John F. Kennedy, Martin Luther King, Robert F. Kennedy, John Lennon and the like.

"But there are also certain public figures who, though less visible, still serve to remind us of who we are and where we've been. Their very presence adds continuity to our history and serves to link one generation to another. Sometimes we don't recognize them until it's too late. And sometimes we do. I felt this shock of recognition . . . when I read that Jacqueline Kennedy Onassis has cancer. Which is to say: the recognition of just how important she is to our brief moment in history."

ooooooo

Jackie's friends did not want to bother her with phone calls. Instead, they sent flowers and notes of encouragement, and followed her progress in the newspapers. They were pleased to read later in February that Nancy Tuckerman was denying reports that Jackie had an advanced case of lymphoma.

"It's not a serious case," said Nancy. "She looks fine and seems fine."

Nancy's upbeat attitude was contagious, and Jackie's friends went around assuring each other, "Don't worry, she's fine."

These friends couldn't imagine Jackie succumbing to cancer. After all, they told one another, Jackie had overcome so many hardships in her life that she would surely triumph over this one, too. The words they commonly used to describe her were "indomitable" and "invincible." It was as though they were describing an immortal.

But Caroline and John were not so sure. They saw their mother getting sicker and sicker by the day. As a result of the chemotherapy treatments, her hair fell out, and she had to wear wigs. She got tired a lot quicker than before.

Ever the responsible mother, Jackie felt it was her duty to cheer up her children, rather than the other way around.

"Don't worry," she said, sounding as chipper as possible. "I'm going to beat it."

On Ash Wednesday, February 16, the family went to the Church of St. Thomas More. A couple of nights before, Monsignor George Bardes had slipped and fallen facedown on an icy street. This day, his eyes were still black and blue as he mounted the pulpit and began to read the gospel to a packed church:

"Do not be like the Scribes and Pharisees who darken their eyes and make it look like they are fasting when they are not. . . ."

The monsignor stopped, looked around, and said, "I didn't darken these eyes. I had a fall the other night."

He was disappointed that his little joke failed to draw the expected laugh from the congregation.

Later, as he walked down the center aisle, he heard Jackie whispering to him, "Father, Father, is there any way I can get ashes privately without everybody watching?"

"Yes," he replied, "just go down the side aisle and walk up to the front, and stand by the altar rail by the last pew, and I'll be back after I greet the people."

Jackie and her children went to the spot designated by the priest. She was pleased and flattered that her children wanted to be with her on this religious occasion. She took great pride in the way Caroline and John had turned out.

"Hers were the only Kennedy kids who didn't spend their summers in Hyannis Port," said a friend who watched Caroline negotiate the shoals of adolescence, and emerge as an attractive young woman. "Jackie kept her kids away from that scene. Her kids didn't get into all that competitiveness; they didn't get into drugs."

Caroline and John escaped the savage, unrelenting afflictions that had struck so many other members of their generation of the family. In 1973, Joseph P. Kennedy II, a son of Robert and Ethel Kennedy, ran his Jeep off the road on Nantucket Island, leaving one of his teenage girlfriends, Pamela Kelly, paralyzed. In 1975, after fifteen-year-old Martha Elizabeth Moxley was brutally slain in Greenwich, Connecticut, suspicion for her murder fell on Ethel Kennedy's nephews, Thomas and Michael Skakel.* In 1984, David Kennedy died of a drug overdose at the Brazilian Court Hotel in Palm Beach. In 1985, Patrick Kennedy, a son of Edward and Joan Kennedy, sought treatment for cocaine addiction. In 1991, William Kennedy Smith, the son of Stephen and Jean Kennedy Smith, was accused of raping a woman at the family's Palm Beach estate; though he was acquitted of the crime by a jury, many people refused to believed that he was innocent.

Of all the Kennedy cousins, Jackie's children were among the few who had escaped the "Kennedy Curse."

∘∘∘∘∘∘

---

*In 2002, Michael Skakel was convicted of Martha Moxley's murder and sentenced to a prison term of twenty years to life.

Jackie felt that Caroline and her low-key husband, Ed Schlossberg, were well matched. Schlossberg, the scion of a wealthy Jewish textile manufacturer, was a former acolyte of Buckminster Fuller, the inventor of the geodesic dome. And Ed was an avant-garde artist in his own right.

"Ed is a designer, conceptualizer, technology guru type who has done a lot of museum exhibits," explained one of his friends. "He's done work on the World Financial Center, Battery Park City, and the ground-floor plaza of the Sony building on Madison Avenue."

What Ed Schlossberg did best, however, was look after Caroline, who had put her career as a lawyer on hold in order to take care of Rose, Tatiana, and Jack.

"Caroline and Jackie see each other a couple of times a week," said one of Caroline's best friends. "Being the daughter of a famous mother has made it hard for Caroline to understand that her problems with her mother are the average person's problems with their mother. On the other hand, I think that Jackie is a woman who knows that she's thin and attractive, and it may not always have been easy for her to relinquish the spotlight to her daughter. Mother-daughter relationships are always complicated, and that can really be the case when it is carried to the grandeur of this particular family."

Caroline's close friend Alexandra Styron, daughter of writers William and Rose Styron, added: "Caroline seems to have come into her own in the last few years. I've never seen her happier than she is now. She looks beautiful. She's stick-thin. Her skin is glowing. She and Ed are as much in love as any married people I've ever seen. They have a very quiet social life. They go out to an occasional dinner party given by a friend. They faithfully go to see friends who are actors in plays. They stick pretty close to home. Caroline is really an extremely unassuming, down-to-earth person."

Caroline had skillfully managed to define herself as her own person, without becoming a superhot media figure. She did not have a bodyguard or a car and driver. She was not on the New York social circuit. She and her husband were friendly with Gail and Arthur Sulzberger Jr., the publisher of *The New York Times.* The Schlossbergs and Sulzbergers were active on the board of Outward Bound.

"Caroline has that wall around her, as does Arthur Sulzberger," said someone who knew them well. "If you are an old close friend, there is no better friend. But she is extraordinarily sensitive to the fact that a lot of people want to be close to her because her name is Caroline Kennedy.

"Given what she has been through," this person continued, "she is as close to normal as circumstances have allowed. She has three nice kids, and raises them as normally as possible. She comes to their private school events in blue jeans. Though she's quite flat-chested, she makes no pretense about it, and wears no padding in her bra. Nor does she wear a lot of makeup. Still, she's gotten a lot prettier as she's gotten older. She's the kind of mother who goes trick-or-treating on Halloween with her kids."

∘∘∘∘∘∘

Jackie never ceased to worry about her children. In my conversations with her, she often expressed her concern for the safety of John and Caroline. Her anxiety was understandable when you recalled that she had lost three other children.

"I sometimes feel as though I'm a kind of Typhoid Mary," Jackie once told me.

Jackie was superstitious, and she feared that Caroline and John lived under the shadow of some terrible Kennedy malediction. Since the assassination of President Kennedy thirty years before, a member of the Kennedy family, or someone closely associated with them, had either died or been the victim of some horrible accident on the average of once every two years.

Though John F. Kennedy Jr. looked like a Bouvier, he was a classic Kennedy daredevil. This naturally gave Jackie cause for concern. She confided to friends, including the author of this book, that John was immature and did not have a clue about how the real world worked. He was also absentminded and accident-prone. For instance, he kept his keys on a chain so that he would not lose them, but when he played with the key chain, he often hit himself in the eye.

If Caroline made Jackie beam with pride, John made her light up.

"Caroline is so focused and dedicated compared with John, who is spread out," Jackie said. "He's a good boy, but he's always getting into a jam. Compared with Caroline, John has a more open personality. But that also means he's more open to stimulation and being led in the wrong directions. I always tell him he's

got to be careful never to do anything that could darken the family name. But I'm not sure he's listening. You never know what he'll do next."

Jackie tended to blame John's difficulties on the fact that he did not grow up with a father. From the psychiatrists she consulted, Jackie learned that the role of a father is to offer his son a vision of what he will become as he emerges into manhood. In order to mature properly, a boy must be presented with an image of what an adult of his gender is like.

And so Jackie sought to compensate for John's lack of a male role model at home by inviting former members of the Kennedy administration to her apartment to talk to John about his father's legacy.

One such visitor was Abraham Ribicoff. A former governor of Connecticut and an ex–United States senator, Ribicoff knew Jack Kennedy from his earliest days in Congress. He was among the first to promote the idea of Kennedy for president. Ribicoff remembered the day in the early 1980s when he was invited by Jackie to speak to John and Caroline about their father.

"Whenever I went to Washington," Ribicoff told them, "I went to your father's office, and your mother would be there. She would always bring him his lunch. He loved Boston clam chowder, and she always brought a pot. He had a lot of health problems, and he had to be careful what he ate. She was the type of wife who'd come with a picnic basket, and there'd always be enough for both him and me. And while we were eating, she'd tell him, 'You're lucky, Jack. If Abe weren't Jewish, he'd be running for president, not you.'"

Later, Ribicoff confided to an acquaintance that he found his talk with John and Caroline one of the most moving experiences of his life.

"You have to remember," he said, "only a few years before, Judith Campbell scandalized the country with revelations about her White House love trysts with President Kennedy and her simultaneous affair with mob boss Sam Giancana. But the children never mentioned her name, and I never alluded to the subject."

oooooo

Until now, Caroline and John had never felt particularly close to Maurice. But after Jackie was diagnosed with cancer, they were deeply touched by the tenderness and care Maurice showed their mother.

"Maurice and Jackie had a great love affair," said one of his oldest friends. "They had very similar interests, except when it came to horseback riding. The both loved the sea, antiquities, cultural entertainment like the ballet. They both gloried in the same thing. They never took each other for granted. Maurice gave up everything else to be with Jackie during her cancer treatment."

Maurice seemed to anticipate Jackie's needs. He understood

that, despite Jackie's wrenching medical ordeal, she needed the company of friends. And he arranged a social life that did not tax Jackie's meager reserves of energy.

One night, Jackie and Maurice had dinner at Lutéce, one of New York's finest French restaurants, with Abe Ribicoff and his wife, Casey. By now, Abe was suffering from the early onset of Alzheimer's disease, but he and Jackie made an effort to be up for the occasion.

"We had a lovely, quiet dinner," Casey recalled. "Jackie and Abe were not well, but we didn't discuss it that evening. We kept everything light."

°°°°°°

Maurice made all of Jackie's appointments under an assumed name at New York Hospital, where she received a course in chemotherapy and steroid drugs.

"It was a cloak-and-dagger operation," said one of Jackie's doctors. "She wanted anonymity, and Maurice made sure she got it."

Secrecy was also employed when Maurice took Jackie to the Stich Radiation Therapy Center for periodic CAT scans. They would arrive at seven o'clock in the morning, before anyone else was there. Jackie often wore a hooded cape and waited outside in the car, while Maurice made sure that no one was in the waiting room. Then he would fetch her and bring her in on his arm.

He always carried a small bag containing Jackie's breakfast, which she usually ate after the CAT scan. However, one morning she could not wait.

"I'm really hungry," she told one of the doctor's assistants. "Would you bring Mr. Tempelsman here?"

"Gee, I hope he hasn't eaten your breakfast," the aide teased. "But I'm sure he wouldn't. He's a special person."

"Oh, yes," said Jackie, "he is."

"Maybe It's Better in Sables"

---

*D*espite the rigors of her treatment, Jackie managed to spend Tuesdays, Wednesdays, and Thursdays in her small corner office at Doubleday. Her first order of business in the morning was to make a list on a piece of paper of famous people and their telephone numbers. Working from the top of the list down, she would call them up and, in her feathery voice, try to persuade them to write their autobiographies.

"I was lucky to be her friend, to have her encourage me and flatter me and never stop asking me through the years to write a book," recalled Aileen Mehle, whose society column, "Suzy," appeared twice a week in *Women's Wear Daily.* "She would call me and write me little notes (I've saved them all) and sit in my apartment and talk. 'You know these people like no one else,' she would say. 'Write about them, their lives, their ambitions, their lies. Write how nothing really is the way it seems. How these women, who seem to have it all, are really desperate and trapped.' Then she would smile and say, 'But if one has to be trapped and unhappy, maybe it's better in sables after all.'"

Jackie succeeded in publishing many books by A-list celebrities—Bill Moyers, Gelsey Kirkland, Judith Jamison, Martha Graham, and Michael Jackson. She would ask these people to do the very thing that she herself would never dream of doing—strip themselves bare in print.

Some of these famous people did not know how to write, and when their manuscripts came in, they were as dense and impenetrable as a rain forest. Jackie had to find ghostwriters to help her untangle the prose.

But she liked being part of the apparatus of a great, big publishing house, and she did not act like a prima donna.

"She really liked to be treated like one of the guys," said a Doubleday associate. "She wanted people to call her Jackie. Her office was smaller than others."

In a rare interview with *Publishers Weekly*, Jackie said, "One of the things I like about publishing is that you don't promote the editor—you promote the book and the author."

Jackie often invited her authors to have lunch with her in her office. They ate out of Styrofoam containers—coleslaw, potato salad, and sandwiches from a nearby delicatessen. If the author was working on a book that required a lot of photos, Jackie would sit on the floor, where she could spread out the photos and rearrange them while she ate.

"Just imagine if *Lifestyles of the Rich and Famous* were covering us now," Jackie joked with one of her authors as they rummaged around the floor. "That would give people out there something to think about!"

The Indian-born author Gita Mehta pointed out that people underestimated Jackie's special talents as an editor.

"I don't think they realize how serious she is," she said. "She's really an extraordinary nineteenth-century type of editor. I watched her do *A Second Paradise*, a book by my brother, Naveen Patnaik. Jackie sent Naveen pages of research material annotated

by herself. It was obscure research. I know as a writer that to have that kind of attention by a commissioning editor is quite rare."

"She edited those books word by word, comma by comma," said another writer. "She knew every detail of every photograph. She knew every detail of the writing. She would telephone you at two o'clock in the morning, saying, 'I'm just calling to check if you're still working on that. Just to see if you're still awake and working.' Or, she'd say, 'I found another phrase where you put in too many adjectives. We've got to get rid of them.'"

Another author who respected Jackie's talents as an editor was the interior decorator Mark Hampton.

"Jackie wrote me and said, 'Why don't you write a book about famous decorators. Time is running out. They're dying off. And you know them all.' And it was true; I had worked with Mrs. Parish, and Billy Baldwin, and Rose Cummings. So I called Jackie, and we decided to do the book, and it was a tremendously amusing experience, and gratifying, because she was a real editor.

"It was called *Legendary Decorators of the 20th Century*," he continued. "It was her idea. She said 'legendary' was a word that always catches people's eyes on shelves in bookstores. And she was very helpful about agreeing who to include, or saying, 'Oh, no, don't put that one in.' And she knew everything about the subject, with only minor exceptions.

"I would turn in my chapters to her, oftentimes late in the week, and I would get them back on Monday with her little penciled, tiny handwriting with that curved writing. And it was terrific to see how good she was at what she did."

° ° ° ° ° °

Jackie was an expert at playing the book-publishing game. She understood how the machinery of a book company worked and what an editor had to do to line up the necessary support inside the organization for her projects.

She actually enjoyed the hand-to-hand bureaucratic combat. When things did not go her way, she did not easily surrender. Her shrewd, tough, practical side came into play. One time, for instance, her colleagues at Doubleday called a meeting to critique a book project she was working on with Tiffany's John Loring.

"Jackie called me," Loring recalled, "and she said, 'We have to psyche them out on this one. You know, we're not going to argue; we're just going to psyche them out. They're going to say this, and I'm going to say that, and then we're going to appear not to agree, and then you're going to say something else, and I'm going to say, Well, you see, we're going to do it this way.'"

"So," Loring continued, "she had done her homework thoroughly and she knew before the meeting what every man and woman was up to, and what they were trying to put over, and who sided with whom, and exactly how to tip the balance at the right moment to get the book the way she knew it should be done."

HOPE

———

$\mathcal{Y}$ou and I have the same mechanism," Jackie told her friend Peter Duchin. "If something unpleasant happens to me, I simply block it out."

They were having lunch in Jackie's apartment, and as often happens with friends who have known each other for many years, the conversation ranged over a wide variety of topics.

At one point, Jackie brought up the subject of Aristotle Onassis.

"Very few people realized how much I loved Ari," she told Peter. "I can't understand it. He was so intelligent in a native way. When his son Alexander died in that plane crash, it changed him as a person. He became impossible to talk to. He was withdrawn and snappish. That was one of the biggest reasons for the dissolution of our marriage."

At another point in the lunch, Jackie expressed her concern about her son.

"Sometimes I wonder if our relationship is a good one," she said. "Sometimes I think I do John more harm than good."

Toward the end of lunch, Peter asked Jackie if he could interview her on tape for the memoir he was writing.

"Oh, I don't think you need tape, do you?" said Jackie, ever-vigilant about her privacy.

But she went out of her way to be helpful to Peter in collecting material for his book.

"When I asked her if she had any memory of my parents," Peter recalled in his memoir, *Ghost of a Chance,* "she replied, 'Only indirectly. But I'll never forget the night my mother and father both came into my bedroom all dressed up to go out. I can still smell the scent my mother wore and feel the softness of her fur coat as she leaned over to kiss me good night. In such an excited voice she said, "Darling, your father and I are going dancing tonight at the Central Park Casino to hear Eddy Duchin." I don't know why the moment has stayed with me all these years. Perhaps because it was one of the few times I remember seeing my parents together. It was so romantic. So hopeful.'"

After Peter transcribed her words in his notebook, he assumed that Jackie was finished. But she continued with a new train of thought.

"You know, Peter," she said, "we both live and do very well in this world of WASPs and old money and society. It's all supposed to be so safe and continuous. But you and I are not really of it. Maybe because I'm Catholic and because my parents were divorced when I was young—a terribly radical thing at the time— I've always felt an outsider in that world. Haven't you?"

"Yes and no," Peter said.

"That's not a bad place to be," Jackie said, smiling.

°°°°°°

Maurice involved himself in every aspect of Jackie's fight against cancer. Because he had learned that cancer patients were often af-

flicted by painful feelings of shame, he encouraged Jackie not to hide from public view.

And so, the two of them ventured forth for daily walks in Central Park. Inevitably, photographers were waiting in the park to record the sight of Jackie in a wig, her face puffy, her step uncertain. On the paths where she had once jogged, Jackie now strolled, leaning on Maurice for support. Once in a while she stumbled, and Maurice had to catch her.

The photographers caught it all, and the pictures of Jackie's physical deterioration shocked many people. Famous women frequently choose to be remembered as they once were, young and vibrant; they guard their image by retreating into seclusion. But curiously enough, Jackie did not seem to mind being seen as frail.

The reason for this was not hard to find. Jackie simply refused to think of herself as a cancer victim. Her doctors had been giving her consistently positive reports: her cancer was being effectively treated. Everything was under control. She was not going to die. And that was all there was to it.

Her display of fortitude and valor touched the hearts of millions, and Jackie became an even more universally beloved figure.

V

Her Enduring Legacy

March 1994

STAYING STRONG-MINDED

*J*ackie noticed that her skin had begun to age; her complexion lost its glow; her face grew gaunt and sallow. In the mornings, when she brushed her hair, huge, frightening clumps fell out. She began wearing a beret to cover the wig.

Throughout the stormy winter of 1994, she fought a fierce battle against the physical and psychological storm raging within her. She became too weak to continue her yoga sessions with Tillie Weitzner. When she took a stroll in Central Park with Maurice, she was unable to go very far before she felt utterly exhausted. When she arrived back at her apartment, she collapsed and went to bed.

She found all this extremely puzzling.

If her cancer had disappeared, why wasn't she feeling better? She refused to contemplate her own mortality. After all, she was only sixty-four years old. By today's standards, that was merely middle-aged. She encouraged Nancy Tuckerman to feed the press optimistic assessments of her progress.

"She's doing so well," said Nancy, who found it harder and

harder to convince herself that what she was saying was true. "She was coming in to a focus group meeting today [at Doubleday], but it was called off because of the snow. She had her grandchildren come over to see her yesterday."

Despite the unmistakable signs of her decline, Jackie continued to promote the image of herself as a woman on the mend. She let it be known that she intended to serve once again as the chairwoman of the American Ballet Theatre's spring gala, and that she would attend the May 9 event in person. She wrote dozens of sunny letters to friends, such as this one to Brooke Astor, the doyenne of New York society:

. . . being with you would make me laugh. The greatest healer. This is your gift. . . . I shall look forward to our doing something together in a little while when all this first part is over. . . .

"She had excellent treatment," said Dr. James Nicholas, chief of surgery at Lenox Hill Hospital and a friend of Jackie's for more than forty years. "Many of the best doctors all around the country were involved."

"She knew a great deal about the immune system," added an oncologist who was part of Jackie's consulting team. "This lady was in no way one of those patients who couldn't digest bad news."

"She learned that the body is different with each person," said a friend. "For instance, she looked specifically into the case of Paul Azinger, the pro golfer who won the PGA in 1993. He had a similar diagnosis of lymphoma. He was having similar treatment. She knew he had been responding. She, too, was a fit person. This should have given her a better-than-average shot. She was cheerful and she stayed strong-minded."

THE SHADOW OF DEATH

It was March 16—the day before St. Patrick's Day—and unseasonably cold. A freezing rain, mixed with sleet and snow, fell on New York City. From the tall French windows of her apartment, Jackie had a spectacular view of the snow-clad city. She could see all the way north to Harlem, south to the Empire State Building, and west to the Hudson River. Directly beneath her window, in Central Park, a few hardy joggers made their way on the icy cinder track that circled the Reservoir. A lone rider, mounted on a black horse, trotted along the bridle path, his head, shoulders, and thighs sheathed in white.

When Jackie emerged from her apartment building at 1040 Fifth Avenue that afternoon, she was wearing her standard "disguise"—a trench coat cinched with a knotted belt, a scarf worn like a babushka and pulled forward to shield the sides of her face, a pair of boots, and her Jackie O sunglasses.

In front of her building, the traffic lanes along Fifth Avenue had been painted green for tomorrow's St. Patrick's Day parade. Police barricades lined the curbs in anticipation of the crowds that were expected to watch the marching bands and floats. Tomorrow, Jackie's grandchildren were scheduled to come to her apartment, where they would have a grand view of the parade from her penthouse window.

The doorman hailed a taxi, and Jackie told the driver the address of Dr. Anne Moore, a renowned cancer specialist affiliated with the New York Hospital–Cornell Medical Center. For the past several weeks, Dr. Moore and the team of eminent specialists treating Jackie had been giving her nothing but heartening news.

After a course of four chemotherapy treatments, all signs of Jackie's cancer had disappeared. Her doctors were greatly encouraged, though their optimism was naturally tempered by the knowledge that her type of cancer—non-Hodgkin's lymphoma—was tough to cure.

Jackie had boundless confidence in her doctors' healing powers. Anticipating good news this day, she had written more upbeat letters to friends, and she asked the taxi driver to stop along the way at a mailbox so that she could drop them off.

One letter was addressed to John Loring at Tiffany & Co. "Everything is fine," Jackie wrote. "Soon we can have another festive lunch."

The second letter was for Niki Goulandris. "I am convinced that everything will turn out well," Jackie wrote.

oooooo

After her examination, Jackie got dressed and settled across the desk from Dr. Moore. The doctor was a pleasant-looking, middle-aged woman whose face betrayed the deep compassion she felt for her cancer patients.

The good news, Dr. Moore told Jackie, was that the cancer had indeed disappeared completely from her neck, chest, and abdomen. . . .

This was the moment Jackie had been praying for, the moment when she would get a clean bill of health.

Dr. Moore continued: All the doctors thought the cancer was gone. . . .

Thought?

Past tense?

But, Dr. Moore said, Jackie's most recent MRI had come back with some very disturbing news. It showed that her cancer had suddenly and unexpectedly spread to the membranes that covered Jackie's brain and spinal cord.

Her cancer had metastasized.

"I can't believe this has happened," said Dr. Moore, who then lapsed into silence.

Jackie, too, was speechless.

For a long time, the two women just sat there, staring at each other without uttering a word.

oooooo

"Of all her doctors, no one saw this coming," said a physician who was intimately involved in Jackie's treatment. "Her doctors were all totally shocked. They thought they had beaten the disease. The whole team was stunned when they got the results of the MRI."

Dr. Moore sent Jackie to see an eminent neurologist at New York Hospital, who confirmed the alarming diagnosis: the cerebellum portion of her brain had been affected.

"Once cancer gets into the brain," the neurologist explained, "it is very difficult to kill with chemotherapy. The brain has a natural barrier that keeps out most chemotherapy drugs."

Next, the neurologist referred Jackie to a neurosurgeon.

"Your best hope of survival is a very sophisticated procedure," he told her. "We drill a hole in the skull, open a shunt, and insert a tube for feeding an anticancer drug directly into the brain. We combine that with radiation therapy to the brain and to the lower spinal cord for about a month."

It sounded horrible.

But Jackie told the neurosurgeon that she was ready to try anything. Two months had passed since Dr. Agresti had informed Jackie that she had non-Hodgkin's lymphoma. And now, for the first time, Jackie found it impossible to hide the truth from herself. She was living under the shadow of death.

Washington, D.C.

Spring 1964

(Thirty years earlier)

Jackie plays tennis with Father Richard McSorley, a Jesuit theologian at Georgetown University, who is counseling her on how to handle her crushing grief. Her deepest regret, she tells the priest between sets, is not having the chance to say good-bye to her husband before he died.

"It was so hard not to say good-bye, not to be able to say good-bye," Jackie says. "But I guess he knew that I loved him."

In her conversations with Father McSorley, which are described in Thomas Maier's book *The Kennedys: America's Emerald Kings,* Jackie makes no secret of the fact that she is thinking of suicide. She feels that she is of no use to herself or anyone else, including her children, Caroline and John.

One time she goes so far as to ask Father McSorley, "Will you pray that I die?"

"Yes, if you want that," the priest replies. "It's not wrong to pray to die."

But suicide, Father McSorley admonishes Jackie, is another

matter altogether. According to the canons of the Roman Catholic Church, suicide is a mortal sin that leads to eternal damnation. If Jackie commits suicide, she will forfeit any chance of being reunited in heaven with Jack Kennedy.

"I know I'll never do it [commit suicide]," Jackie tells Father McSorley. "I know it's wrong. It's just a way out."

"Why Me?"

---

*N*ow, thirty years later, Jackie felt that her life was spinning out of control again.

As the child of a broken home and the survivor of two rocky marriages, Jackie had struggled to gain mastery over her fate. And, until recently, she thought she had succeeded. Today she had a thriving career as a book editor at Doubleday; she was rich beyond her wildest dreams; she had a steadfast companion in Maurice Tempelsman; she had two devoted children, and three healthy grandchildren.

These last few years had been the best years of Jackie's life—better by far than her years as the powerful consort of the president of the United States, or the pampered spouse of one of the richest men in the world, Aristotle Onassis. She had managed to preserve her dignity—and sanity—through an ordeal with the press such as no other woman in the twentieth century had ever endured.

Despite all the terrible tragedies that had befallen her, Jackie had not only survived, she had triumphed. Her life was now so full of peace and contentment that she found it impossible to believe that it was all about to be snatched away.

"Cancer is an unsettling reminder of the obdurate grain of unpredictability and uncertainty and injustice—value questions, all—in the human condition," wrote Dr. Arthur Kleinman, in *The Illness Narratives*. "Cancer forces us to confront our lack of control over our own or others' death. Cancer points up our failure to explain and master much of our world. Perhaps most fundamentally, cancer symbolizes our need to make moral sense of 'Why me?' that scientific explanations cannot provide."

○○○○○○

As part of her new treatment, Jackie had to take large doses of prednisone, a powerful anti-inflammatory steroid. Almost immediately, her face began to change. It became full and red—characteristics of the Cushing's syndrome that resulted from the administration of steroids. She experienced terrible headaches, back pain, and muscular weakness. Some days, she "crashed" and couldn't get out of bed. Other days, she experienced feelings of grandiosity and invulnerability. She had a fierce appetite, which no amount of food seemed to satisfy.

"The moment I realized there was really something wrong with her was the last time we ate lunch at Le Cirque," said John Loring. "Sirio Maccioni [the owner of the restaurant] loved to send over a sampling of desserts after lunch. Jackie would never touch them. She might stick her fork in and eat two crumbs and say, 'Isn't that wonderful,' and that was the end of that.

"She was obviously not looking terribly well, but she was in a wonderful mood, and we were having a good time. And at the end of lunch, the usual four or five desserts appeared, covering the whole table.

"And she said, 'You start that one. I'm going to start this one.'

"And she actually started to eat this dessert. And I thought, Well, that's remarkable.

"So I said, 'You're not going to finish that, are you? I'm going to have the waiter take this away right this minute.'

"She said, 'If anyone tries to touch one of those, I'm going to stab them in the hand with my fork. I'm going to eat every single one of them.'

"And she did. We sat there and plowed through every single dessert on the table. It was astonishing, but it was also terrifying, because it was like she had decided that this was not going to work out, and so why not eat all the desserts on the table. She might as well eat everything if she wanted to."

Praying for a Miracle

Whenever she left her apartment, Jackie was set upon by hordes of paparazzi. Their photos of a shockingly feeble Jackie were published all over the world, enabling millions of people to witness the spectacle of Jackie withering away bit by bit.

It was a distressing sight, a painful reminder of human frailty. Of all the women in the twentieth century, Jackie had been the supreme embodiment of youthful glamour. Even after she turned sixty, and had begun to show signs of aging, she was still viewed as a romantic symbol of the golden age of Camelot.

Now, as if anticipating her obituary, stories began to appear in newspapers and magazines assessing her role in history. Though she was widely admired, she was generally given little credit for any enduring achievement, unless one counted her contribution as a mother who had raised two "normal" children. Indeed, Jackie was often depicted as a pre-feminist symbol who, for all her fame and glamour, lived in the shadow of powerful men.

"Over the years," wrote the historian Carl Sferrazza Anthony, "there was scant mention in the press of Mrs. Onassis's substantial accomplishments. . . . Three decades after adults saw a Jackie impersonator open *The Jack Benny Show* and children saw Jackie Kennelrock on *The Flintstones,* thirty years after Jack-E-Lantern masks were popular at Halloween and Miss America swooned 'If only I looked like Jackie' at her crowning, the press still clung to 'The Jackie Look'—so much so that it made a reappearance on fashion runways in the early 1990s (which she found 'silly').

"The mystique theory was kept alive, even at the cost of factual documentation, in part because it had become the media's most enduring, not to mention most lucrative, cottage industry. As the years went by, Mrs. Onassis herself rarely discussed— certainly never in print or live interviews—the many accomplishments she did succeed in making, but which the public would not, it seemed, acknowledge."

○○○○○○

This omission said more about America's celebrity-saturated culture, and its elevation of myth over reality, than it did about Jackie. The fact was, Jackie played a far more significant role in the White House than she was given credit for.

"She was a young woman of notable beauty, at once wistful and luminous, and of acute intelligence and exacting expectations," wrote Arthur M. Schlesinger Jr., who served as a special assistant to President Kennedy and knew Jackie from her earliest days in the White House. "She had been reared in a class, a time—the 1940s—and a place—Newport, Rhode Island—where young ladies were taught to conceal their brains lest they frighten young men away. She observed upper-class conventions, but underneath a veil of lovely inconsequence she developed a cool assessment of people and an ironical slant on life. One soon realized that her social graces masked tremendous awareness, an all-seeing eye, ruthless judgment, and a steely purpose.

"Jacqueline Kennedy brought several unusual qualities with her to the White House," Schlesinger continued. "One was a knowledge of the arts. Her response to life was aesthetic rather than intellectual or moralistic. . . . To her appreciation of the arts [she] added a passionate sense of history. She liked to know how things began and how they evolved, and her glamorous modernity was based on an intense curiosity about the past."

If the most important job of a first lady (a title that Jackie despised) was to help win the public's endorsement of the president and his political agenda, then Jackie had to be ranked among the most successful first ladies in history. With her magnetic star quality, Jackie drew millions of supporters to her husband's cause and, in the last days of his life, became his most important political ally. In this respect, at least, she was the equal of Eleanor Roosevelt and Hillary Rodham Clinton.

"I soon learned that Mrs. Kennedy's wish, murmured with a 'Do you think . . .' or 'Could you please . . .' was as much a command as Mrs. Eisenhower's 'I want this done immediately,'" wrote J. B. West, chief usher at the White House, in his memoir, *Upstairs in the White House*. "In public, she was elegant, aloof, dignified, and regal. In private, she was casual, impish, and irreverent. She had a will of iron, with more determination than anyone I have ever met. Yet she was so soft-spoken, so deft and subtle, that she could impose that will upon people without their ever knowing it."

Jackie left behind a record of accomplishments for which she alone could take credit. Before she moved into the White House, Americans were accustomed to looking across the ocean to Europe for cultural nourishment. In transforming the White House into a glittering showcase for famous American artists, Jackie was responsible for helping to awaken the country to its own rich cultural heritage.

By restoring the White House, helping to save Lafayette Square, and fighting to preserve the Old Executive Office Build-

ing, Jackie was a major impetus behind the historic preservation movement, which changed the entire face of urban America.

Jackie persuaded President Kennedy to ask Congress for substantial funding for the arts. She was a leading force behind the creation of the National Endowment for the Arts. Thanks in large part to Jackie, the notion that government should take a leading role in promoting the arts became a permanent part of the American cultural landscape.

"Washington had always been a company town, dominated by government and politics, and Jacqueline Kennedy wanted to make it, like Paris and London, the cultural as well as the political capital," wrote Arthur Schlesinger Jr. "The Eisenhower administration had endorsed proposals for a national cultural center, and Mrs. Kennedy hoped for something along the lines of Lincoln Center in New York City. The project became in due course the John F.

Kennedy Center for the Performing Arts and has given new salience to the arts in the republic's capital."

"By late 1963," added Carl Sferrazza Anthony, "the stage was set for the realization of her biggest goal: the creation . . . of the equivalent of the first Cabinet post for the arts. President Kennedy was going to sign an executive order appointing aide Richard Goodwin as the first Special Assistant to the President for Cultural Affairs. But fate and tragedy intervened: Kennedy was scheduled to sign the order on November 22 aboard Air Force One, after a stop in Dallas. It was still in his briefcase when he died."

Many upwardly mobile Americans identified Jackie with French sophistication. "For a certain middle-class segment of the population," wrote cultural historian David M. Lubin in *Shooting Kennedy: JFK and the Culture of Images,* "preparing and eating French food and drinking French wine became a means of achieving liberal sophistication. . . . "

Nor would history forget the impact that Jackie had on generations of American women. After her failed marriage to Aristotle Onassis, she could have continued to live the life of a pampered rich woman. Instead, she chose to become a working mother, a decision that had an immense influence on millions of women who longed for a profession of their own, but who, like Jackie, did not want to sacrifice their femininity.

"Jackie had these traditionally 'masculine' qualities—she was smart and loved intellectual pursuits, she was knowledgeable about history and the arts, she wore pants, and she had big feet," wrote media historian Susan Douglas. "Yet she was still completely feminine, a princess, a queen. She knew how to take charge, and yet she also knew how to be gracious and ornamental."

In 1964, a year after she left the White House, Jackie tried to persuade Defense Secretary Robert McNamara to stop the Vietnam War.

"She had a great sense of compassion," McNamara said. "She

was horrified by violence, particularly violence done in war, and particularly the Vietnam War. I recall her pleading with me to stop the violence. She literally beat on me physically with her fist once when I was having dinner with her in New York. She was saying, 'This killing must stop!'"

In the last decade of her life, Jackie could no longer be described as a woman who played a supporting role in the lives of powerful men. She declared herself fully liberated when she chose to invite her companion, Maurice Tempelsman, to live with her without the benefit of marriage.

She was, at last, the chief actor in her own drama.

○○○○○○

As winter slowly surrendered to spring, Jackie spent more and more time praying in the Church of St. Thomas More.

She arrived there in the late afternoon, when no one else was around. She wore a scarf covering the sides of her face and (even on cloudy or rainy days) her big sunglasses.

She found an unobtrusive place in the back and to the side of the empty church. Occasionally, she looked up from her kneeling position and stared at the large gold cross, which was missing the crucified figure of Christ. His body had taken leave of his soul. Just as Jackie's body would soon be separated from her soul.

"As a parishioner, she came to worship often, almost always incognito," said Monsignor George Bardes. "Sometimes, you wouldn't even know she was in the church.

"She was a very religious person. How could she be otherwise, given all the tragedies that have befallen her?"

"Jackie," said a family friend, "was fascinated with the life hereafter—especially reincarnation. She once said to me, 'I'm sure I'll have to go through many lives, and many heartaches, before I become perfect in a new life.'"

In a letter to Niki Goulandris, Jackie revealed that she was praying for a miracle. While kneeling in church, she told Niki, her mind often wandered to other times, and other churches, and other dying people. In particular, she remembered how she and Niki were together in Paris when Aristotle Onassis was dying, and how they went to Notre Dame Cathedral and prayed together for his recovery.

Now, Jackie wrote Niki, she had an even more important incentive to pray. She wanted desperately to live, not only for herself, but also for her grandchildren, whom she loved above all other creatures on earth.

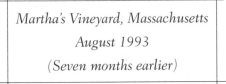

Martha's Vineyard, Massachusetts
August 1993
(Seven months earlier)

Caroline's daughters, Rose and Tatiana, spend the month of August on Martha's Vineyard with Grand Jackie. One of the highlights of the stay is their visit to Gus Ben David, director of the Felix Neck Wildlife Sanctuary on the shore of Sengekontacket Pond. Gus extends a special invitation to Mrs. O (as he calls her) and her granddaughters to see his eagles, owls, hawks, boa constrictors, alligators, and turtles.

This day, Jackie, Rose, and Tatiana pile into a Jeep driven by Albert Fisher, Jackie's caretaker, and set off for the sanctuary. Five-year-old Rose is the most excited, for she is partial to snakes.

When they arrive, Gus is waiting for them in his usual attire: a khaki shirt with a blue lapel button that says AUDUBON SOCIETY. He is a warm, outgoing, fifty-year-old native Vineyarder who is good with children. Gus has spent the last twenty-nine years visiting local schools and educating children about wildlife.

"Jackie loved to come to the sanctuary," Gus says. "We had a mutual interest in wild, living things. Where she owned property in Gay Head—that whole place is extraordinary, in itself a wildlife sanctuary. She loved her property. All the deer, ducks, and swans there. I put an osprey pole on her property so that the birds could nest. Animals were a rich part of her life."

As he has before, Gus leads Rose, Tatiana, and Grand Jackie on a tour of the sanctuary. First, they visit the fascinating educational displays. Then, Gus takes out his fifty-five-pound common snapping turtle, which was caught by Albert in Squibnocket Pond adjacent to Mrs. O's property. The girls love the turtle, who is named

Big Al. They scurry after it as it trudges along the grass. At one point, Mrs. O bends down and pets the turtle on its carapace.

But Mrs. O seems to like the birds better. She tells Gus how glad she is that he takes care of them so well.

Then comes the pièce de résistance—a visit to Gus's snakes. The 250-pound African and Burmese pythons are too big to take out of their pens, but Rose handles the smaller snakes—green anacondas, an albino snake, a boa constrictor, and a Texas indigo.

Next, they move on to the baby alligator, the savannah monitor lizard, the golden eagle, and the African bullfrog.

They spend an hour or so, and then it is time to leave.

"From the moment she arrived to the moment she left," says Gus, "Jackie never stopped asking questions and laughing. She had as much fun as Rose and Tatiana. She had such enthusiasm for everything living. She was just like a kid herself."

VI

Making a Small Masterpiece

April 1994

INTO THE FIRE

With the shocking news that her cancer had spread, Jackie could no longer pretend that everything was going to turn out all right. It was now unmistakably clear that she had little time. But her reaction was not at all what her doctors had expected. Characteristically, Jackie's response to death was the same as it was to life—aesthetic rather than rational.

To understand how Jackie's mind worked, it was necessary to go back several decades, to 1951, and Jackie's senior year in college, when she won *Vogue* magazine's annual Prix de Paris contest. First prize was a six-month internship in *Vogue*'s offices in Paris.*

Jackie was asked to write an essay on "People I Wish I Had Known." At the time, Jackie was struggling to break away from the stifling dependence on her mother, and her essay reflected her struggle to identify with her unconventional father.

While other applicants chose women like Madame Curie or

---

*Jackie's mother, fearing that Jackie might never return from Paris and marry the rich man she had in mind for her, persuaded her daughter not to accept the prize.

Eleanor Roosevelt, Jackie chose three highly unconventional male artists: the French poet Charles Baudelaire, the Irish author Oscar Wilde, and the Russian ballet impresario Sergei Diaghilev.

Jackie described them in terms that she could easily have applied to her father, who always talked about raising life to an art form. Baudelaire and Wilde, she wrote, "both were poets and idealists who could paint sinfulness with honesty and still believe in something higher." As for Diaghilev, "though not an artist himself, he possessed what is rarer than artistic genius in any one field: the sensitivity to take the best of each man and incorporate it into a masterpiece all the more precious because it lives only in the minds of those who have seen it and disintegrates as soon as he is gone. . . .

"If I could be a sort of Overall Art Director of the Twentieth Century, watching everything from a chair hanging in space," she concluded, "it is [the theories of Baudelaire, Wilde, and Diaghilev] that I would apply to my period, their poems that I would have music and painting and ballets composed to."

o o o o o o

More than forty years later, Jackie still subscribed to this aesthetic vision. Aware that her life would soon be over, she consciously set out to give artistic shape and purpose to her final days. She aspired to make her own death nothing less than a small masterpiece.

She had no intention of taking her own life; that would be a mortal sin in the eyes of the Church, and bar her from joining Jack Kennedy in heaven. However, as weak as she was, she intended to "art direct" events from that metaphoric chair hanging in space.

And so, on the Monday after Easter, she began setting things in motion. She reviewed her living will, which stated that her doctors were not to use extraordinary measures to keep her alive. She held a final discussion with her attorney, Alexander Forger, about her last will and testament, in which she directed her children,

Caroline and John, to help maintain in death the privacy that she had so fiercely guarded while alive.

Jackie planned to leave the bulk of her estate, which was worth nearly two hundred million dollars, to the C&J (Caroline and John) Foundation, a charitable-lead trust designed to last for twenty-four years.

"In a charitable-lead trust," wrote Susan E. Kuhn of *Forbes* magazine, "a set amount of money is distributed to charities each year and, at the end of its term, the remaining assets are passed on to a named beneficiary. Jackie's will names Caroline, John, Maurice, and Alexander Forger as trustees, and directs them to give an annual amount equal to 8 percent of the initial net fair market value of the assets to charities, preferably those 'committed to making a difference in the cultural or social betterment of mankind, or the relief of human suffering.' Twenty-four years hence, the assets pass to her grandchildren."

Jackie went through the books in her library, picking out a few favorites as gifts for friends and doctors. And she summoned her old friend Nancy Tuckerman to her apartment.

When Nancy entered the library, she found Jackie curled up on a sofa in front of a roaring fire, surrounded by her books and music. Jackie was wearing a chenille sweater and a pair of slippers. A glass of iced tea was within easy reach. Nancy noticed the absence of the distinctive red pack of Pall Malls that had never been far from Jackie's side. After forty years of smoking, Jackie had finally quit.

On the table beside her were stacks of letters representing a lifetime of personal correspondence. The letters were neatly bound with ribbons. Jackie tugged at the end of one of the ribbons, and a letter fell onto the astrakhan that covered her lap. The letter was nearly forty years old, and the paper on which it was written was brittle. She read the letter out loud to Nancy.

"Dear Jacks . . ."

The letter was from her father, the roguish "Black Jack" who was the archetype of all the men Jackie had fallen in love with.

Her father's letter was very tender and personal, and when she finished reading it, Jackie tossed it into the fire.

In no particular hurry, she picked up another letter, read it out loud, then consigned it to the flames, too. One by one, she chose which letters to save and which to incinerate. She had a reverence for history, but she also had to decide just how much she wanted to reveal about herself after she died.

Which was not very much.

Unlike many other former first ladies, Jackie had never kept a diary. The author David Wise, who worked with her on his 1987 novel *The Samarkand Dimension,* once asked her if she would ever consider doing her memoirs. In view of her eagerness to publish the memoirs of other notable people, Jackie's response was puzzling.

"Maybe when I'm ninety," Jackie said flippantly. Then she turned more serious: "People change. The person you might have written about thirty years ago is not the same person today. The imagination takes over."

As an example, Jackie mentioned one of her favorite books, Isak Dinesen's memoir, *Out of Africa.* "Dinesen," Jackie said, "left out how badly her husband had treated her. She created a new past, in effect. . . . And why sit indoors with a yellow pad writing a memoir when you could be outdoors?"

Her respect for privacy extended to others as well. During her life, practically every man who had met Jackie fell under her spell, and many of them had written her indiscreet letters. She felt a responsibility to protect these men, as well as their wives and children.

And there were things about her private life that she had never told her children, and that she preferred they didn't learn about after she was gone.

There was, for instance, a passionate letter, dating from the 1950s, from the writer John Marquand Jr., Jackie's first great love.

It went into the fire.

And there was another letter, equally ardent, from Rear Admiral Guerin, the French naval attaché in Washington during the Kennedy administration. At the time, there had been rumors that Jackie and the dashing French admiral were carrying on an affair.

The rumors were true, and the letter went into the fire.

And another letter, this one from Gianni Agnelli, the heir to the Fiat automobile fortune, a notorious playboy, an avowed hedonist, and Jackie's paramour for a short time in the summer of 1962. Gianni wrote to Jackie in Italian about a night they had spent together aboard his eighty-two-foot yacht, where they had danced barefoot on the deck to a five-man mandolin band.

Into the fire.

And there was a letter from John Warnecke, the brilliant architect who designed President Kennedy's grave site at Arlington National Cemetery. A couple of months ago, Warnecke, who was now in his late seventies, had read in a newspaper about Jackie's battle against cancer, and he had sent her a Valentine's Day card.

"I still love you," Warnecke wrote.

Into the fire.

Hyannis Port, Massachusetts
November 1964
(Thirty years earlier)

John Carl Warnecke, a third-generation California architect, is forty-five years old and at the height of his personal and professional powers. A former college football star, he is a ruggedly handsome man who shares Jackie's passion for design, architecture, painting, and nature.

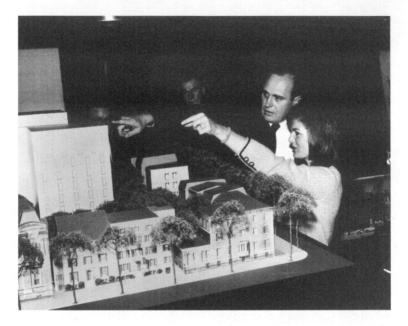

At the end of the summer of 1964, he is ready to complete the project for which Jackie has chosen him: President Kennedy's grave site. All that remains is to pick the stone that he will use for the engraved words of the president's inaugural address.

Warnecke has found a stone carver in Newport, Rhode Island, and a few weeks before the first anniversary of the assassination, he is ready to ask Jackie for her final approval.

Meanwhile, Jackie's mother, Janet Auchincloss, has been thinking a lot about Jackie's future. Her daughter's year of mourning is almost up, and it is time for her to get on with her life. Jackie needs a husband. And as far as Janet can see, Jack Warnecke—well-spoken and well-mannered—is made to order.

This weekend, Jackie drives down to Newport from her home in Hyannis Port with two Secret Service agents. After lunch, Warnecke takes her to inspect the stonecutter's work. She loves it. The approval of the stone means a great deal to both of them.

"It was really the turning point in our relationship," Warnecke says. "Now I could schedule a press conference, and formally announce that the design had been approved before the first anniversary. It put a close to Jackie's year of mourning."

When they get back to Hammersmith Farm, the Auchincloss house in Newport, Jackie announces that she plans to return to Hyannis Port the next day.

"Why don't you dump the Secret Service and let me drive you back?" Warnecke says.

"That would be great, Jack," Jackie says.

"I had learned early how to handle the Secret Service," Warnecke says. "Those guys liked and trusted me, because I had once been a football player, a jock, and one of them."

The next day, Jackie and Warnecke get into her black Mercury convertible, put down the top, and head off for the Cape. The Secret Service follows at a discreet distance. When they arrive at Jackie's house in Hyannis Port an hour and a half later, Jackie's housekeeper, Marta, tells her that she has arranged for Caroline and John to spend the night at another house in the Kennedy compound.

"We were alone," Warnecke says.

Jackie shows Warnecke her collection of landscape paintings by André Dunoyer de Segonzac. Warnecke admires the seascapes that she has done herself. They have dinner, then Jackie gives him a tour of the rooms upstairs.

Warnecke's head almost hits the sharply slanted ceiling in Jackie's bedroom. He stands with Jackie for a few moments at the window, looking out at the choppy waters of Nantucket Sound. Then, wordlessly, he leads her over to the bed that she once shared with Jack Kennedy, and they begin to make love.

Afterward, Warnecke tells Jackie that he loves her.

"I fell in love with you the first moment I saw you," he says.

"I love you, too, Jack," she says.

A Noble Spirit

When Jackie was finished burning her letters, she and Nancy sat in silence, watching the hearth grow cold, until only a few small glowing embers remained in the heaps of flaky gray ashes.

Nancy did not know what to make of the scene she had just witnessed. How could a woman like Jackie, who had such respect for history, destroy important historical documents?

But then, Jackie had always been a mystery to her friends—and not simply because she was disposed to secrecy and concealment. On the contrary, whenever Nancy went to Jackie's apartment for dinner, Jackie revealed the most intimate details of her life. She spoke freely and openly about all sorts of things—her sex life, her children's problems, her views of other famous people. She did so with the expectation that friends like Nancy would behave like priests in the confessional, binding themselves to a sacred oath of silence.

Of course, Jackie did not rely solely on the good intentions of her friends. She possessed the means of enforcing her wishes. She had the power to grant or withhold immense social cachet through her friendship. Her first inkling of this power came in the White House.

"It gradually dawned on her that she had all these people fighting for a smile, fighting for a nod of approval," recalled her personal couturier, Oleg Cassini. "Some days, when she was in a good mood, she was the most fantastic, charming person. But I was at parties where she would barely say hello to you—she was mad at you because you didn't do something according to Hoyle.* She began to be aware that she might go down in history as one of the great women of the period."

Jackie wielded her friendship the way a medieval monarch might employ her royal sword; she could choose to either dub you a knight of her Round Table or cut off your head.

Anyone who betrayed Jackie's trust was instantly banished from her kingdom. And since few people were willing to risk such social obloquy, Jackie's confidences were guarded with religious zeal.

But knowledge of Jackie did not necessarily lead to an understanding of Jackie. She was like quicksilver, constantly changing her form and shape, forever undefinable.

Aaron Shikler, who painted the portrait of Jackie that hung in the White House, said: "I did many, many studies of her for what many people would say was a gloomy portrait—it was very intense. And when I started to do it full-size I said to myself, 'It's not right—it's got to be a little lighter, more open.' That's when I started the one that's in the White House, but she preferred the first version. Then, when she made her decision to marry Onassis,

---

*Edward Hoyle, an eighteenth-century English writer, wrote a book of rules for card games and "according to Hoyle" has come into the language to mean rules accepted as standard or authoritative.

it was like something disappeared. She relaxed, became girlish, giggly. It was like another person working with me."

∘∘∘∘∘∘

"As soon as Nancy Tuckerman announced that Jackie had cancer, I called Jackie immediately," said Niki Goulandris, Jackie's Greek friend. "I told her, 'I'm leaving for the United States immediately. I'm coming to New York to see you.'

"But she assured me not to bother.

" 'It's all under control,' she said. 'Not to fear.'

"I remember she told me that John had just come back from Central America, and that I had to go to the virgin forests there.

"After that, I received one or two letters from her. Each time she wrote the same thing: 'I am convinced that everything will turn out well.' She was a very religious woman. More so than even Catholics priests appreciated. When she first came to Skorpios with her children, when they were very young, they all went to an Orthodox church on the mainland of Lefka. There was no Roman Catholic church nearby.

"For her, art and culture were part of God's revelation. Art and culture connected her with something beyond our earthy concerns. She had a mystical quality. She believed in things that could not be put into words. That's how she explained all the remarkable events in her life—in a deep mystical sense.

"And she always mentioned God in her letters. She would write, 'I'm praying for this person and that person, for this to happen and for that to happen.' She did not live life without a deep belief in God. She believed in a providential plan.

"The last thing I heard came from Nancy Tuckerman. I had sent Jackie a nice Byzantine icon, because I knew this would touch her religious sense. Jackie no longer had the strength to write, and she asked Nancy to take over that burden."

Dear Niki:

. . . Jackie hopes you will understand why she is not writing you herself. Right now, the doctors want her to concentrate on gaining back her strength after her operation. . . .

With my love,

Nancy

Once a week, Caroline and her nannies brought Rose, Tatiana, and Jack to Jackie's apartment to play with Grand Jackie.

"With her flagrant imagination," Nancy said of Jackie, "she was able to hold their attention for hours on end. There was this enormous red wooden chest in which she kept all sorts of hidden treasures for them: pirate loot, Gypsy trinkets, beaded necklaces, rings with colored stones.

"As soon as they arrived," continued Nancy, according to Christopher Andersen's *Sweet Caroline*, "everything from the chest was dumped out on the bedroom floor, and the children would dig in. They'd deck themselves out with jewelry and put on costumes they'd made from old scarves and odd bits of material. Jackie would then take them on a so-called fantasy adventure. She'd weave a spellbinding tale while leading them through the darkened apartment, opening closet doors in search of ghosts and mysterious creatures. Once they were finished playing, they'd have their traditional afternoon tea party sitting on the living room floor."

○○○○○○

Ten days later, on Wednesday, April 13, a cold, hard rain beat down on the canopy in front of Carly Simon's apartment building. Jackie ducked out of a taxi and scurried inside. She had been invited to lunch at Carly's sprawling apartment on Central Park West.

When Jackie got off the elevator, she saw that Carly had left her front door open. Jackie walked inside. Though Jackie truly loved Carly, her friend's decorating taste offended her aesthetic sensibilities. Carly had never outgrown her 1960s hippie period; she favored native crafts, bright pillows, and woven shawls. Half of the living room was taken up with music equipment and microphones for a band.

Jackie and Carly first met in the early 1980s at the Ocean Club, a popular restaurant on Martha's Vineyard. They hit it off at a dinner party given by Rose and William Styron, who had a house on the Vineyard.

"When she got back to New York, Jackie called me and asked me to write a book," Carly recalled. "She liked artistic people who were free spirits, people who could make her laugh.

"Once at lunch in the Cafe des Artistes on West Sixty-seventh Street, she was a half-hour late," Carly continued. "I got into a panic, because I thought something awful had happened to her. When she arrived, she told me that she had been trapped in an elevator. And she said to me, 'You're like a Thoroughbred, so finely tuned.' I think she meant that I was high-strung, and that she was tougher than I was. But what she liked about me was my emotional availability, my availability to discuss my feelings with her."

Carly's other lunch guests—Joe Armstrong, the publisher; Peter Duchin, the band leader; and Duchin's wife, Brooke Hayward—greet Jackie warmly. There is one person in the room Jackie has never met: the talented documentary filmmaker Ken Burns, who was in the process of editing his Public Broadcasting System series on the history of baseball. Carly was featured on Burns's sound track singing "Take Me Out to the Ball Game."

Over lunch, Jackie asked Burns a lot of questions about his

project. But Burns could only stay for part of the lunch. After he had left, someone asked Jackie how she was feeling.

"Only four more weeks and I'll get my life back," she said, referring to this round of chemotherapy. But, she added, reverting to the third-person pronoun, "One does not look forward to a summer on the Vineyard with a bad wig."

"We didn't have a conversation about her battle with cancer," said Peter. "We all knew she was ill. She was very brave about it. Of course, we didn't go into any detail. I remember her saying she got tired a lot quicker. But she was very chipper. And she said, 'I am going to beat it.'"

Someone else asked Jackie about her sister, Lee.

"She stopped by for tea," Jackie said.

"Do you see her often?"

"We've only seen each other once this whole year," Jackie said. "I guess she called me so she could say that she saw me. I never could understand why Lee is so full of animosity."

After lunch, on Jackie's way out, Carly handed her a big, folded piece of paper.

"I want to give this to you," Carly said. "I wrote it for you."

It was the lyrics of Carly's new song, "Touched by the Sun," the last lines of which went:

I, I want to be one
One who is touched by the sun, one who is
touched by the sun.

The next day, April 14, was sunny and dramatically warmer. Marta threw open the windows to air out the apartment. Jackie sat in the library, making phone calls and enjoying the fragrant spring breeze that wafted through the room. She called Carly Simon twice, both times thanking her effusively for the lyrics to "Touched by the Sun."

Then, suddenly and without warning, Jackie collapsed. Marta

phoned Maurice, who told her to call an ambulance. Jackie was rushed to the hospital, where surgeons operated on a perforated ulcer—a complication of the steroid therapy. To Jackie, who had endured so much over the past few months, the painful stomach surgery was the last blow.

∘∘∘∘∘∘

When she came out of the hospital late in April, Jackie's attitude had changed. She told Maurice that, while she still had the mental capacity, she wanted to write notes to her children, to be read after her death.

Maurice helped her sit up in bed. He brought Jackie her robin's-egg-blue stationery and a vintage black-and-gold-trimmed French fountain pen, which had belonged to her late father. As she began to write, her loping, girls'-school handwriting degenerated into a messy, almost illegible scrawl.

Dear John,

I understand the pressure you'll forever have to endure as a Kennedy, even though we brought you into this world as an innocent. You, especially, have a place in history.

No matter what course in life you choose, all I can ask is that you and Caroline continue to make me, the Kennedy family and yourself proud.

Stay loyal to those who love you. Especially, Maurice. He's a decent man with an abundance of common sense. You will do well to seek his advice.

Love,

Mummy

Dear Caroline,

The children have been a wonderful gift to me and I'm thankful to have once again seen our world through their eyes. They restore my faith in the family's future. You and Ed have been so wonderful to share them with me so unselfishly.

Love,

Mummy

Maurice helped Jackie fold the notes and stuff them into their envelopes. She labeled one "John," the other "Caroline," then licked and sealed both.

Then Jackie settled back into her pillows and closed her eyes. While she slept, Maurice sat by her side, holding her hand.

VII

Her Way

May 1994

THE UNBREAKABLE TRINITY

I don't think I can take it anymore," said Jackie, who had been readmitted to the hospital on May 16 with shaking chills.

The burden of living had become too much for her. The doctors who had promised she would experience minimal pain turned out to be wrong. She suffered from pounding headaches, the result of her brain cancer. As a side effect of the steroids, which lowered her resistance to infection, she contracted pneumonia. Every breath was agony. The powerful narcotic dripping into her veins made her nauseated. And then there was the terrible mental anguish that went with knowing that waves of malignant cells were dividing geometrically inside her body, doubling every few days, eating her alive.

"Let us know what you want," one of Jackie's doctors advised. "We can try experimental medications and procedures. It's a matter of how much you want to go through."

She did not want to end her days the way many cancer patients ended theirs: lying on stiff, bleached sheets in an ugly, antiseptic hospital room, connected to tubes, but disconnected from friends, family, and cherished belongings.

She picked up the rosary that had been placed within easy reach and fingered its cold, hard beads. She tried to recall what the French nuns had taught about saying the rosary.

"Make the sign of the cross and say the Apostle's Creed; say the . . ."

But her memory failed her.

She was gradually losing what the doctors called "mentation"—the ability to think. Her mind was shutting down along with her body. But she still experienced brief moments of lucidity when she remembered that she believed in God, the father of mercies, and in his promise of eternal life, and that she and Jack would soon be reunited in heaven.

". . . say the Our Father; say three Hail Marys . . ."

There! She had remembered it, after all!

She began saying the rosary in a low, hoarse whisper. She said it all, then she said it again. And when she was finished, she felt grateful to the French nuns, and forgave them for their heartless cruelty.

She was ready to leave this mortal coil.

°°°°°°

At Jackie's bedside in the hospital, Caroline and John tearfully begged her to fight on, not to give up. Since their father's assassination, there had been just the three of them, an unbreakable trinity. They could not imagine life without one another, especially without their mother. They pleaded with her to take more antibiotics to combat the pneumonia.

"As John sat on the edge of Jackie's bed holding her hands in his, she was quietly crying and saying they had to be strong," said one of the nurses. "When John came out of her room, he leaned against the wall. His eyes were red. He pressed the fingers of his right hand to his lips and touched the door of his mother's room. It was like a last kiss."

From time to time, doctors came into Jackie's large corner suite, which overlooked the sludgy East River and the Queensboro Bridge. When the hospital assigned her to this room, suite 1619, she had noticed the plaque beside the door—THE STAVROS NIAR-CHOS SUITE—and had been amused by the irony. The suite was named after Aristotle Onassis's shipping archrival.

The nurses took her blood pressure and temperature. Then, one of her doctors leaned over the bed, and gave her another devastating piece of news.

Her cancer had spread again—this time to her liver.

"Caroline was sitting beside Jackie's bed, holding her hand," said a member of the hospital staff who was in the room. "John was standing on the other side of the bed stroking his mom's forehead. Jackie's face was deathly pale, her cheeks hollow.

"When the doctor broke the terrible news, there was stunned silence. Then Jackie sighed deeply in resignation. Caroline cried out, 'Oh, my God, no!' and burst into tears. She cradled her mom in her arms, and Jackie began crying, too.

"John walked over to Maurice and Ed Schlossberg, who had been standing at the foot of the bed, and the three men put their arms around each other."

Dr. Moore said, "Let's try more chemotherapy."

"No, no," Jackie said. "I want to go home to die."

A GOOD DEATH

----

*O*ver the strenuous objections of both family and doctors, Jackie discharged herself from New York Hospital early on the afternoon of Wednesday, May 18.

It was a damp, cool day, in the low sixties. Showers were predicted. Jackie was bundled up as an orderly wheeled her stretcher to an exit. Even though it hadn't started raining yet, Maurice held a black umbrella over the stretcher as Jackie was lifted into a waiting ambulance. Maurice and a nurse rode in the back with Jackie, while the hospital transfer director rode in front with the driver.

Jackie was utterly exhausted. Maurice held her hand as the ambulance headed up York Avenue for the ten-minute ride to her apartment.

"You're a good and loving man, and you've made these years so wonderful," Jackie told Maurice. "I will always be with you in spirit. I love you. Now, hold my hand and let me rest as we ride home together. I feel so tired. . . ."

oooooo

Jackie had always been conscious of her place on the stage of history, and once she arrived back at her apartment at 1040 Fifth Avenue, she prepared for her farewell performance. She was determined to have a good death—a humane, merciful ending.

Such a death required a great deal of preparation, as well as the cooperation of others. Caroline helped her make a list of close friends and family members who would be permitted to enter her bedroom chamber to say their last good-byes. Maurice arranged for round-the-clock nurses, and a morphine drip with a PCA—a patient-controlled anaesthetic button, which allowed Jackie to administer an extra pulse of pain medication if she needed it. However, since it was against Dr. Moore's medical ethics to permit a patient to assist in her own death, there was a lock on the morphine drip, limiting the number of milligrams per hour, so that Jackie could not kill herself, intentionally or not.

Jackie went over all the details of her funeral. She told her children and Maurice that she had considered having her body cremated and her ashes scattered so that people couldn't turn her grave site into a garish tourist attraction. But she had decided against that, choosing instead to be buried at Arlington National Cemetery next to Jack Kennedy.

"I was the president's wife," she explained, "and the country would expect me to be buried there. I can't escape that responsibility."

She wanted her funeral to be held at the Church of St. Thomas More, but it turned out that the church could accommodate only three hundred and fifty people—less than half the number Jackie planned to invite. She agreed to have the funeral service moved to the far larger St. Ignatius Loyola Church, a ninety-six-year-old neoclassic limestone structure on Park Avenue and Eighty-fourth Street, where she had been baptized as an infant and confirmed as a teenager.

The Reverend Wallace Modrys, the pastor of St. Ignatius Loyola, would preside at the mass and give the homily. Uncle Teddy would deliver the eulogy. John would call Jessye Norman and ask her to sing some hymns. There would be readings by John, Caroline, Maurice, and two of Jackie's best friends—the director Mike Nichols and the writer Jane Stanton Hitchcock.

Flowers would be handled by the flawless Bunny Mellon. John Loring of Tiffany & Co. could be counted on to oversee the proper wording and printing of the funeral invitations. George Trescher, the savvy society events-planner, would draw up the seating plan, have the invitations hand-delivered, and handle any last-minute glitches.

There was one point on which Jackie and Teddy, who was consulted by phone, did not see eye to eye: to what extent the funeral service should be public. Speaking for his mother, John told Father Modrys that they wanted everything extremely private. Senator Kennedy, on the other hand, wanted it more public.

"The sticking point was whether there should be a live TV broadcast from inside the church," recalled Father Modrys. "The senator wanted it. John didn't. I put in my two cents. I thought it would be appropriate to have a loudspeaker broadcast the audio portion of the services outside the church, but not to allow TV cameras inside. It took a little while for the family to give us clarity on what their wishes were."

Nonetheless, Jackie realized that a lot of important political figures would likely attend her funeral. She said that she wouldn't be surprised if Lady Bird Johnson, who was infirm and rarely seen in public, made the effort to come. Another first lady, Hillary Rodham Clinton, would certainly want to be there, as would New York's senior senator, Daniel Patrick Moynihan, and two other senators who had known and loved Jack Kennedy—John Glenn of Ohio and Claiborne Pell of Rhode Island.

Then there was the Kennedy clan to think about. The Kennedys would be out in full force—Teddy would see to that—

and Jackie was terrified that an assassin, dressed as a priest, would slip past the police lines and get into the church. Security had to be drum-tight.

It was difficult for Jackie to concentrate on all these details. Now that the cancer had invaded her liver, that organ was failing to clear the toxins from her blood, which made her drowsy and sleepy. She felt as though she had taken too many Valiums.

Nonetheless, she gathered her last ounce of strength and, with the help of the ever-faithful Marta, chose a set of her favorite floral sheets. She picked out a nightgown and a scarf to cover her head, which had become totally bald from the chemotherapy treatments. And finally, she selected the Gregorian chant ("Alleluia, Beatus Vir Qui Suffert") that would be piped through the apartment on the CD player in the closing moments of her life.

REPOSE

---

*T*hat same afternoon, May 18, Bunny Mellon arrived at Jackie's
apartment. She was greeted at the door by Maurice Tempelsman,
who was unshaven and looked as though he had not slept in days.
Maurice had practically given up his diamond business to stay
near Jackie and take care of her.

"I was in Antigua when Jack was killed," Bunny told Maurice,
"and I wasn't immediately available to Jackie. I never forgave myself, and I didn't want that to happen this time."

"We weren't worried about you," Maurice said. "We knew
you'd be here. Jackie's waiting for you in her room."

On the way back to Jackie's bedroom, Bunny found Caroline
in her old childhood room. She lay on the bed, fully dressed, her
eyes closed, crying. Bunny did not disturb her.

She knocked softly on Jackie's door, then entered. The walls of
the room were pale lime green. Jackie was propped up in a beautiful coral-red canopy bed. Books were everywhere. The only other
person in the room was a nurse, who monitored the morphine
drip beside Jackie's bed.

Bunny sat next to Jackie and took her hand. She leaned over and whispered in such a low voice that the nurse could not hear what she said. After a while, Bunny got up, lit some candles, took a CD out of its case, and put it into a player. The Benedictine monks of Santo Domingo de Silos were heard chanting "Alleluia, Beatus Vir Qui Suffert."

Alleluia, alleluia,
Blessed the Man who stands the proof,
Because once he is tested
He will receive the crown of life.
Alleluia!
Alleluia, alleluia.

Bunny suggested to John, who was wandering aimlessly around the living room and library, that he order food from a caterer. Then she went to find Marta to ask her to phone a few of Jackie's closest friends and invite them to come as soon as possible. Calls went out to socialite Jayne Wrightsman, Carly Simon, and Peter Duchin and his wife, Brooke.

"Marta called and asked if we'd like to see Mrs. Onassis, who was quite ill," said Duchin. "It seemed a bit too theatrical to me. Knowing Jackie so well, I knew that it was the opposite of what she'd have wanted. For her to say a last good-bye to everyone, while people were making jokes in the living room—a kind of pre-death viewing, if you will—struck me as medieval."

Not everyone saw it that way. As soon as Carly Simon got the call, she and Joe Armstrong rushed over to Jackie's building. When they arrived, thousands of people had already gathered on the street in front of 1040 Fifth Avenue. The police did not have time to set up barricades, and people spilled off the sidewalks on both sides of Fifth Avenue. Red double-decker tourist buses went by

every few minutes, loudspeakers blaring with the announcement that they were passing the residence of former first lady Jacqueline Kennedy Onassis.

It was a circus. Traffic came to a standstill. Rubberneckers tried to see what was going on. Television captured the whole hysterical scene via huge satellite transmitters on the tops of trucks, and beamed it around the world.

000000

Upstairs in Jackie's apartment, John welcomed the visitors as they stepped off the elevator into Jackie's foyer. Caroline was too distraught to talk. She sat on a bench in the gallery, softly crying on the shoulder of her husband. Family members—Lawfords, Kennedys, and Shrivers—roamed around the apartment, which was filled with the sounds of Gregorian chant.

"Except for Maurice and John, and some other male members

of the family," said Carly, "only women were being allowed in the bedroom. One of Jackie's last wishes had been that none but a few women friends outside the family be permitted to see her at her time of dying."

Carly entered the room; Bunny was sitting on a chair by the bed, holding Jackie's hand.

"You sit with her now," Bunny said to Carly.

Carly exchanged places with Bunny and looked at Jackie.

"Jackie was unconscious," Carly said. "She had a print scarf over her head. She was under the sheets. There was an intravenous needle in her arm. In repose, her face was completely smooth and translucent. Her mouth was slightly open, and there was the sound of a delicate exhalation. As the Gregorian chants continued to play, various members of the Kennedy family filtered in and out of the room. Everybody was talking in hushed tones.

"I felt privileged that the family had allowed me to be in the room with Jackie. I spoke to Jackie in a low and comforting voice, telling her how much I loved her. Maurice stood at the end of the bed, observing. Bunny, not far away on a settee, was praying.

"During the time I was sitting with Jackie and holding her hand, I felt as though I had a direct communication with her—an experience that was deep, personal, and untainted by self-consciousness. And as I opened the door and left the room, and walked through the halls, and said good-bye to the family members, I started crying."

º º º º º º

Throughout the night of May 18, Caroline, John, Maurice, and Bunny took turns at Jackie's bedside. They read passages aloud from her favorite poets—Robert Frost, Emily Dickinson, and Edna St. Vincent Millay.

From time to time, Jackie became conscious of the presence of others in the dimly lighted room. She looked up at Caroline's and John's faces, which were lined with grief and a lack of sleep.

"It's late," Jackie whispered. "Go home and get some sleep. . . ."

When she woke in the morning, Jackie summoned her priest, Monsignor Bardes, to give her the last rites.

"Caroline and John wanted to put off the holy anointing until later," the priest said. "They didn't want to accept that these were their mother's final hours."

It was a little past eleven in the morning when Monsignor Bardes entered Jackie's bedroom and pronounced the traditional words of greeting that began the ritual of extreme unction: *"Pax huic domui."* He put on his stole, genuflected, and rose. He took the holy water and sprinkled Jackie in the form of a cross, then the floor and walls. Then he leaned his ear close to Jackie's lips, and heard her confession.

"Bless me, father, for I have sinned."

"May the Lord be in your heart and help you to confess your sins with true sorrow. . . ."

oooooo

As the hours went by, family members filed into Jackie's room two by two—Ethel and Pat, Eunice and Sargent Shriver, Jean and her son William Kennedy Smith. In the evening, just before Jackie slipped into a final coma, Ted Kennedy entered the chamber.

"Ted knelt by her bedside," said a family member who was in the room. "He told Jackie emotionally, 'I know there have been times you've been disappointed in me. . . .' But before he could go any further, Jackie held up a hand and stopped him.

"She said, 'Ted, you always did your best to hold this family together, and I've always respected you for that. What I want for you is to enjoy the rest of your life with your wife, Victoria.'"

Ted was too overcome with emotion to speak. He just nodded his head, gave her a loving hug and left the room in tears.

○○○○○○

Shortly after 10:15 P.M. on May 19, John, Caroline, Maurice, and Bunny emerged from Jackie's bedroom.

"Mother's dead," John told the other members of the family. "She passed away peacefully. She just slipped away."

Ted Kennedy suggested that someone go downstairs and issue a public statement to the press. But Caroline bristled at the suggestion.

"We don't owe them anything," she said, full of bitterness over the deathwatch outside her mother's building.

But cooler heads prevailed. The next morning, May 20, John, dressed in an impeccably tailored navy-blue suit, emerged from the lobby of 1040 Fifth Avenue and faced the press.

"Last night, at around ten-fifteen, my mother passed on," John said. "She was surrounded by her friends and family and her books and the people and things that she loved. And she did it in her own way, and on her own terms, and we all feel lucky for that, and now she's in God's hands."

AFTERWORD

*H*er death was front-page news everywhere.

The New York Times ran one of the most remarkable obituaries in its 143-year history. It began under a three-column headline on the front page and continued inside the paper for two full pages, with no fewer than ten photographs illustrating the major events and personalities in Jackie's life.

The newspaper treated Jackie as a major historic figure. And it assigned one of its most graceful wordsmiths, Robert D. McFadden, to do her justice.

Although she was one of the world's most famous women—an object of fascination to generations of Americans and the subject of countless articles and books that re-explored the myths and realities of the Kennedy years, the terrible images of the president's 1963 assassination in Dallas, and her made-for-tabloids marriage to the wealthy Mr. Onassis—she was a quintessentially private person, poised and glamorous, but shy and aloof.

The historian Michael Beschloss went even further. Interviewed on television, he maintained that Jackie was one of the two most important first ladies of the twentieth century, the other having been Eleanor Roosevelt. Many commentators praised Jackie for her bravery in the face of crushing tragedy. And everyone seemed to agree that Jacqueline Bouvier Kennedy Onassis died as she had lived—in her own inimitable fashion.

oooooo

Two days after Jackie's death, on Saturday, May 21, Eunice Kennedy Shriver kept a long-standing commitment and gave the commencement address at Loyola College in Baltimore. Among the Kennedy clan, Eunice was considered to be the smartest member of her generation. Her father, Old Joe Kennedy, once remarked, "If Eunice was a man, she'd be president instead of Jack."

Now, Eunice eulogized Jackie:

"For us—and to my wonderful and big, extended family—Jackie always reminded us that loyalty to one another was to be fiercely practiced and protected. To America, she embodied the beauty of art, of music, of design, and, more than anything, the beauty of family. These were her gifts to us and to the world. . . ."

oooooo

At the request of Teddy Kennedy, Caroline and John agreed to hold a wake in their mother's apartment. Her body was placed in a burnished mahogany casket that matched the natural color of her hair. Covered with white flowers and green leaves, the casket was displayed in her living room, near the gray draperies and under the chipped plaster on the ceiling.

Late on the afternoon of Monday, May 23—four days after Jackie's death—the first of more than one hundred guests began to arrive. Carly Simon was accompanied by her husband, Jim Hart, and a shiatsu masseuse named Biko, who had known Jackie quite well.

"Biko brought a gift, a long candle in the shape of a calla lily," Carly said. "And I brought the lyrics to my song 'Touched by the Sun,' which I had written out on parchment and tied with a pretty silvery ribbon.

"We walked inside," Carly continued. "There were tons of people, all in high spirits. Lots of laughter. It was a traditional Irish wake, and it turned me off. It was like walking into a cocktail party.

"Bunny Mellon was there. So were all the Kennedys. And Daryl Hannah, who had her arms folded across a beautiful cashmere sweater in a defensive posture, and who looked really uncomfortable. Jayne Hitchcock, the novelist, was there with her new boyfriend, Jim Hoagland, the Pulitzer Prize–winning journalist. The director Mike Nichols was in the crowd. And, of course, Maurice."

Monsignor Bardes of the Church of St. Thomas More, who had been asked to speak at the wake, recalled: "The apartment was filled with people, senators, celebrities. Caroline received everyone. It was so hot and crowded that someone fainted, and a doctor had to bring them around.

"Jackie's aunt, Maud Davis, who had come down from Connecticut, was a bit worried how she would be received," the priest continued. "There had been friction between Jackie's family and Maud's. But before she died, Jackie had written Maud a letter, saying, 'Often as I lie here, I wish I were back with all our family, including you, in East Hampton, where we spent so many wonderful summers.' Caroline grabbed and hugged Maud, and said, 'How glad I am to see you.' All was forgiven that day. Many misunderstandings were corrected. It was all just about love."

Someone in the crowd came up to Maurice and said in a voice that was loud enough to be heard over the din, "She was so wonderfully lucky to have had you for those years." And Maurice replied, "No, I was so wonderfully lucky to have had her."

"I couldn't get over everybody's high spirits," Carly Simon said. "I had such a heavy heart. They felt the loss, too, but they spoke a different language than I did. The Kennedys are Irish, and they accept death in a different way.

"There was a tiny kneeling place in front of the casket. Biko said that we were supposed to leave our offerings—the candle and the parchment—on top of the casket. So we went and got them and placed them on top, and knelt and prayed.

"Caroline's husband, Ed Schlossberg, came over. He said, 'We're very angry with you, Carly. You have to take those things off the casket. It's only for the grandchildren.' He went on and on in this vein—how intrusive it was, what I had done. 'You committed a faux pas,' he said.

"I was crying as I left. On my way to get my coat, Bunny Mellon met me. 'Don't worry,' she said. 'I'll take care of it. I'll make sure Jackie gets your gifts.'"

○ ○ ○ ○ ○ ○

The next morning, Tuesday, May 24, a procession of black limousines pulled up in front of St. Ignatius Loyola Church on Park Avenue. Politicians, popular entertainers, and other famous personalities emerged from the cars, squinting in the bright spring sunshine. Just as Jackie had predicted, Lady Bird Johnson, silver-haired and on a cane, put in an appearance, slowly climbing the stairs leading into the church.

The white flowers and green leaves that had covered Jackie's coffin were removed, and in their place a dark-red and gold brocade coverlet was placed over the shiny mahogany wood. The coffin was borne by eight pallbearers, among them some family members, including William Kennedy Smith.

The stretch of Park Avenue in front of the church was closed to traffic, and the police were on high alert. They had been warned by their supervisors to be on the lookout for a man masquerading as a priest. Everyone was mortally afraid that an assassin would slip through the police lines and murder a member of the Kennedy family.

The tight security kept spectators behind barricades several hundred yards away. According to Jackie's wishes, television cameras were not allowed inside the church. But the audio portion of the service was broadcast live on radio and television, and it was also carried by outdoor loudspeakers facing Park Avenue.

"There was a lot of pressure," said the Reverend Modrys, who referred to Jackie during his homily in the French manner, pronouncing her name *zhak-LEEN*. "One of the tensions I felt was to keep the focus, not on the celebrity moment, but on this woman, with so many close friends and family members. I wanted to protect the integrity of the moment, so that it didn't become a circus. There was a danger that things could spin out of control.

"The Kennedys maintained security inside the church, so there were no gawkers," Father Modrys went on. "Otherwise, you would have had ten thousand people. We couldn't accommodate that number. And by gawkers, I mean priests and others, too. Like my little niece, who was only interested in whether Arnold Schwarzenegger was there, and whether I shook his hand."

The only member of the media allowed inside the church was Jackie's old friend Aileen Mehle, aka the society columnist Suzy.

"I turn[ed] to watch Ethel [Kennedy] as she walked up the aisle, bent, pale-faced and heavy-hearted, surrounded by her sons and daughters," Suzy wrote a few days later. "How many times has she taken these devastating steps before? Too many. On the podium, Jackie's beautiful children, Caroline and John [spoke] lovingly of their mother; Jackie's friend, Jayne Hitchcock . . . recited the Twenty-third Psalm; Mike Nichols [told] of Jackie's spirit of adventure. . . ."

Jessye Norman sang a pair of hymns, Franck's "Panis Angelicus" and Schubert's "Ave Maria." And Maurice read one of Jackie's favorite poems, "Ithaka," by the Alexandrian Greek, C. P. Cavafy.

When you start on your journey to Ithaka,
then pray that the road is long,
full of adventure, full of knowledge . . .

That the summer mornings are many,
that you will enter ports seen for the first time
with such pleasure, with such joy! . . .

Always keep Ithaka fixed in your mind.
To arrive there is your ultimate goal.
But do not hurry the voyage at all.
It is better to let it last for long years . . .

After the service, members of the family boarded a chartered jet at La Guardia Airport and took Jackie's body to Washington, D.C. From there, the funeral procession made its way to Arlington National Cemetery, where some one hundred people gathered in a summery breeze in front of the eternal flame that Jackie had lit three decades before in honor of her assassinated husband.

The simple, eleven-minute ceremony was conducted by the Reverend Philip M. Hannan, the retired Roman Catholic archbishop of New Orleans and an old family friend, who had presided at John F. Kennedy's funeral. Among the distinguished mourners was the president of the United States.

"We say good-bye to Jackie," said Bill Clinton. "May the flame she lit so long ago burn ever here and always brighter in our hearts."

Then, Jackie was laid to rest next to President Kennedy and two of their children—a baby girl who had died in birth and the two-day-old Patrick Bouvier. As the mourners bowed their heads, sixty-four bells rang out from the tower of the Washington Cathedral across the Potomac River—one bell for each year of Jackie's life.

First Caroline, then John knelt to kiss their mother's coffin. Caroline moved back, but John stepped over to his father's gravestone, and bent and touched it.

ooooo

While Jackie lived, the three most important people in her life—her children and Maurice Tempelsman—had gotten along famously. Once she was gone, however, things were never quite the same.

Several months after Jackie's death, John let Maurice know that he would like to have his mother's apartment to himself while renovation work on his recently purchased loft in TriBeCa was being completed. He gently suggested to the older man that he find his own place to live, which Maurice did by moving to the Sherry Netherlands Hotel, which was located twenty-five blocks south on Fifth Avenue.

However, neither John nor Caroline wanted to live permanently in Jackie's apartment, and they created quite a sensation when they put it on the market.

"I remember someone who looked at the apartment, and said, 'Oh, it's in such terrible shape,'" recalled the designer Mark Hampton. "I thought to myself, 'They don't get it.' It was just in the shape she left it. It was immaculate and the floors were shiny, shiny. But it hadn't been painted in decades. That was what she loved. That's what a lot of people love.

"I think that has great charm, that look," he continued. "I admire it. And I think one of the critical aspects of her taste and her eye is the fact that her style didn't change. The rooms she decorated as a young woman in Georgetown and in their private rooms in the White House were very little different really in substance to the way some of the rooms at 1040 Fifth Avenue looked thirty years later.

"And it was the same with her clothes, you know. You can see pictures of her all through those decades. She never looks out of style. You never look at a picture and say, 'Oh, how dated this picture looks!' Never. Her house never looked dated. She never looked dated."

Eventually, the apartment was bought by oil tycoon David Koch and his socialite wife, Julia, for $9.5 million. They announced plans to gut the apartment and completely rebuild it, which they did at a cost of another several million dollars. Since Caroline and John did not have room for many of their mother's possessions, they sent them to Sotheby's for auction.

"Caroline knew that I was familiar with Jackie's household belongings," said Hampton, "so she asked for my help. I had a lot of things restored and recovered that had to be fixed before the auction."

Maurice was not in favor of the auction.

"He didn't try to stop the auction," said one of Maurice's closest friends, "but he didn't like the idea. He told me, 'I don't want to see Jackie's possessions on public display. But the kids like the idea. If it was up to me, I'd sell the stuff privately.'"

But John ignored Maurice, as he did his advice about flying. John began to take lessons at the FlightSafety Academy in Vero Beach, Florida.

"I worry about John flying," Maurice told a friend. "He's so distractable."

As the years wore on, Maurice continued to see Caroline and John at meetings of the trustees of Jackie's estate, and at the annual Profile in Courage Awards at the John F. Kennedy Library and Museum in Boston. Otherwise, they saw very little of one another.

○○○○○○

As I have written in another book, death spared Jackie the unbearable anguish of learning that her beloved son perished in a plane crash. In that sense, death did her a great favor.

But that has not stopped people from asking, "What would have happened if Jackie had won her heroic six-month battle against cancer? What if, by some miracle, she had not died at the age of sixty-four? What if, instead, she had lived on—for another ten years, or fifteen years, or perhaps even longer?"

Of course, Jackie would have enjoyed watching her grandchildren grow up. And she would have derived immense pleasure from growing old with Maurice. But that is merely stating the obvious.

Of far greater interest to Jackie's legion of admirers is a more complex question: "If Jackie had lived, would she have made a significant difference in the lives of other people?"

Naturally, we can only speculate on the answer to such a question. But as someone who had the opportunity over the course of a dozen years to observe Jackie and talk with her about many things, I believe the answer is "Yes."

For starters, consider this: Had she lived and met Carolyn Bessette, Jackie would most probably have disapproved of John's choice of a mate.

How do I know that?

Jackie was a shrewd judge of character, and she would have seen Carolyn for what she was—a rather shallow, psychologically unstable young woman who spelled trouble for her son.

As Jackie's old friend Arthur Schlesinger Jr. put it: "Jackie developed a cool assessment of people . . . [a] tremendous awareness, an all-seeing eye, [a] ruthless judgment. . . ."

In my view, Jackie would have done everything in her power to prevent her son from marrying Carolyn. And although we cannot be sure of such things, it seems inconceivable that John would have taken such a monumental step and married Carolyn against his mother's expressed wishes.

Thus, it does not stretch the imagination to speculate that had Jackie learned about John's secret plans to become a pilot and his desire to marry Carolyn, she would have raised objections to both. And reluctantly or not, John would have listened to his mother as long as she was alive.

It was Jackie's death that "liberated" John, and offered him the freedom to pursue his own destiny. Within a few short months of his mother's funeral, John ended his four-year affair with Daryl Hannah, began living with Carolyn Bessette, started *George* magazine, and got his pilot's license.

"For the first time, no one was telling John what to do," said Sue Erikson Bloland, the daughter of famed psychoanalyst Erik Erikson, and a psychotherapist in her own right. "It is understandable that he would choose such a wife as Carolyn Bessette, someone who replicated Jackie's function in his life by making decisions for him and making him feel cared for."

Indeed, John talked openly about the freedom he felt after his mother's death.

"We were talking about losing your parents," recalled Lisa De-Paulo, who wrote articles for *George,* "and John said something that I will never forget. He said, 'There is something liberating, as weird as that sounds, to being parentless. With the loss comes an odd sense of liberty. You find yourself making decisions. While your parents are alive, there is always unconditional support, but you always feel the need to please them.'"

According to his Uncle Teddy, John had serious plans to run for public office—most probably for governor of the state of New York. Teddy privately told friends in the Democratic Party that the governor's mansion in Albany would be the best possible stepping-stone for John on the road to the presidency—and a restoration of the Kennedy dynasty.

A number of astute political observers agreed. The presidential historian Michael Beschloss, for example, believed that John had "a sort of post-modern political sensibility—a grasp of the fact that politics . . . is heavily larded with celebrities, that we're living at a time where especially young people are skeptical about politicians. He was trying to fashion an approach to politics that allowed him to sort of get across the old Kennedy ethic of public service and idealism, but to do it in the new vernacular of Generation X. And had he run for president in the twenty-first century, I think that, to some extent, would have been the basis."

In a conversation that John had with David Pecker, the head of the U.S. division of Hachette Filipacchi Magazines, the company that bankrolled and distributed *George,* John revealed his interest in pursuing a life in politics.

"He told me that his only job interest was the governorship of New York State," said Pecker. "The senate was too much work. 'You know me, David,' he said, 'I don't want to work so hard.'

"He was kidding, of course, about hard work," Pecker continued. "But believe me, the Republicans looked on John Kennedy as a very serious challenger to New York's governor George Pataki. I was at a magazine advertiser's event in Florida—a fragrance organization—and I had a chance to talk to Pataki personally about it. And he told me, and I quote, 'The only person I'm afraid of when I run for reelection is JFK Jr.'"

Everyone agreed: John was golden. He was blessed with every asset imaginable. He had the looks, the presence, the charisma. He could do anything in life he wanted. There was only one qualification: his mother had to stay alive in order for John to live, too.

o o o o o o

And so, in the end, it turned out that the life and death of Jacqueline Bouvier Kennedy Onassis mattered very much indeed. Her loss had major consequences for her children, the Kennedy family, the Democratic Party, and the nation.

Ten years after Jackie succumbed to cancer, it is hard to believe she is dead. In our imagination, she is still very much with us. She was supposed to go on forever—an immortal who taught us how to live.

She was not supposed to teach us how to die.

> *Middleburg, Virginia*
> *November 1993*
> *(Six months earlier)*

On November 19, 1993—the day before Jackie fell from her horse—she and Charles Whitehouse enter in a point-to-point race. No one knows Jackie better than Charlie Whitehouse. Their mothers were friends before either Charlie or Jackie were born, and they have been close ever since they can remember. Charlie and Jackie have a great deal in common, including their good manners, deep sense of responsibility, and passion for horses.

Charlie has entered them in the race as an "older team," a term that Jackie doesn't like. But the fact is that when she reaches the finish line, she is badly out of breath.

Charlie has never seen her like this before, but he does not suspect that there is anything seriously wrong with her. After all, Jackie appears to be the picture of health. She can barely suppress her excitement over the prospect of participating the next day in the Piedmont hunt.

That reminds Charlie of a story, and he reminisces about a time that he and Jackie went foxhunting in a tremendous downpour. He asked her rather hopefully if she didn't think it would be a good idea to get out of the rain and go inside. And he vividly remembers what Jackie replied.

"Oh, not yet, Charlie," she said. "We're already wet and, who knows, something wonderful might happen."

ACKNOWLEDGMENTS

*W*riting is solitary work, but publishing is a team effort. For *Farewell, Jackie,* I was fortunate to have two of publishing's best players on my team—the formidable literary agent Dan Strone of Trident Media Group and the brilliant editor Molly Stern of Viking Penguin. To them I owe a special debt of gratitude for helping me shape the book you now hold in your hands.

I also wish to thank my photo researcher, Melissa Goldstein, who has an encyclopedic knowledge of Jackie images; Betsy Parker, an equestrian reporter who taught me about the sport of foxhunting, and conducted several interviews on my behalf with Jackie's friends in the Virginia hunt country; and Carolyn Coleburn, who launched this book through her untiring publicity efforts.

NOTES

*E*ven now, ten years after her death, Jacqueline Kennedy Onassis remains something of an enigma to her fans, her friends, and even to her own family.

Jackie was able to maintain an air of mystery by making it clear to all who came near her that, as I have written, she expected them to behave like priests in the confessional and bind themselves to a sacred oath of silence. Anyone who betrayed Jackie's trust was banished from her kingdom.

This fear of being cut off from Jackie while she was alive still inhibits some people from talking now that she is dead. However, most human beings have a compelling need to speak about what they know. And so, over the course of more than fifteen years, I have interviewed several hundred people about Jackie. Many of these interviews have been on the record. But many others were conducted on condition of anonymity.

INTRODUCTION

Brief passages on Jackie's death can be found in *The Kennedy Women* by Lawrence Leamer (Villard Books, 1994); *Jackie, Ethel, Joan: Women of Camelot* by J. Randy Taraborrelli (Warner Books, 2000); *Sweet Caroline* by Christopher Andersen (William Morrow, 2003); and the author's *Just Jackie: Her Private Years* (Ballantine Books, 1998).

I. THE REAL JACKIE

The descriptions of daybreak in the Virginia hunt country, Jacqueline Kennedy Onassis's riding attire, and the Piedmont foxhunt are based on reporting done on the author's behalf by the respected equestrian journalist Betsy Parker, who conducted interviews with several of Jackie's friends and fellow riders.

The material on Jackie's appearance, her personal habits (smoking, nail-biting, diet, physical exercise, yoga, etc.), and her anxiety regarding the anniversary of John F. Kennedy's assassination are drawn from the author's own observations of Jackie as well as from notes of his conversations with her.

Insights into Jackie's religious and spiritual feelings are based on interviews with Monsignor George Bardes as well as with several other priests who wish to remain anonymous.

Other author interviews for this section include Dr. Bernard Kruger, Sheila Sisk, Rachel Lambert "Bunny" Mellon, John Loring, I. M. Pei, Michael Beschloss, and Mark Hampton.

Books that were used in this section include Christopher Andersen's *Sweet Caroline;* Frank Brady's *Onassis, an Extravagant Life* (Prentice Hall, 1977); Lester David's *Jacqueline Kennedy Onassis: A Portrait of Her Private Years* (Birch Lane, 1994); John H. Davis's *The Bouviers: From Waterloo to the Kennedys and Beyond* (National Press Books, 1993); Peter Evans's *Ari: The Life and Times of Aristo-*

tle Onassis (Diamond Books, 1988); Frieda Kramer's *Jackie* (Grosset and Dunlap, 1979); Katharine Graham's *Personal History* (Vintage, 1988); C. David Heymann's *A Woman Named Jackie: An Intimate Biography of Jacqueline Kennedy Onassis* (Orion Publishing Co., 1995); Mason Houghland's *Gone Away* (The Derrydale Press, 2000); the author's *All Too Human: The Love Story of Jack and Jackie Kennedy* (Pocket Books, 1996) and *Just Jackie;* David E. Koskoff's *The Mellons: The Chronicle of America's Richest Family* (Ty Crowell Co., 1978); Laurence Leamer's *The Kennedy Women;* Paul Mellon's *Reflections in a Silver Spoon: A Memoir* (William Morrow, 1992); Jerry Oppenheimer's *The Other Mrs. Kennedy* (St. Martin's Press, 1995); Jean Stein and George Plimpton's *American Journey: The Times of Robert Kennedy* (Harcourt, 1970); J. Randy Taraborrelli's *Jackie, Ethel, Joan;* William Wright's *All the Pain That Money Can Buy: The Life of Christina Onassis* (Orion Publishing Co., 1992); and James L. Young's *A Field of Horses: The World of Marshall P. Hawkins* (The Derrydale Press, 1995).

Background on Bunny Mellon and her relationship with Jackie was gleaned from interviews by the author and his research assistants with Hélenè Arpels, Robin Duke, Peter Duchin, Mark Hampton, Kitty Carlisle Hart, John Loring, and Paul Leonard, and with others, who wish to remain anonymous.

Some of the ideas in this section were expressed in a different form by the author in previous books on Jacqueline Kennedy Onassis—*All Too Human* and *Just Jackie*—as well as in the author's article "Jackie, Yo!" in the August 1989 issue of *Vanity Fair.*

Other sources include the Associated Press, November 25, 1993; "Unraveling the Mortal Coil, in Plain View," *The New York Times* "Week in Review," October 19, 2003; "Remembering Jackie . . . ," *Town & Country,* July 1994; Martin Filler's "Cool Mellon," *Vanity Fair,* April 1992; Judith Thurman's "Costume of the Country," *The New Yorker,* May 14, 2001; "Lasting Impressions," *Washingtonian,* May, 1994; "Oak Springs Splendors," *House*

Beautiful, June 1998; "Paul Mellon's Gift," *House Beautiful,* July 1997; Mac Griswold's "The Art Works That Paul Mellon Couldn't Part With," *The New Yorker,* February 15, 1999; "Mrs. Mellon's Secret Garden," *House & Garden,* June 1988; "The Jacqueline Kennedy Garden," *House & Garden,* October 1984; and "Guest Speaker: Paul Mellon," *Architectural Digest,* August 1993.

Newport, Rhode Island, September 12, 1953
(Forty years earlier)

The description of Jack and Jackie's wedding day, which appeared in a different form in the author's *All Too Human,* comes from interviews with Hélenè Arpels, Hugh Auchincloss III, James Auchincloss, Betty Beale, Marion "Oatsie" Charles Leiter, Taylor Chewning, Philip and Cecilia Geyelin, Sylvia Whitehouse Blake, Evelyn Lincoln, Chauncey Parker, Ellen D'Oench, George Smathers, Paul "Red" Fay, Charles Spalding, James Reed, and Nina Auchincloss Straight.

Books that were used in this section include Stephen Birmingham's *Jacqueline Bouvier Kennedy Onassis* (Pocket Books, 1979); Diana DuBois's *In Her Sister's Shadow: An Intimate Biography of Lee Radziwill* (St. Martin's Press, 1997); Peter Collier and David Horowitz's *The Kennedys: An American Drama* (Encounter Books, 2001); C. David Heymann's *A Woman Named Jackie;* John H. Davis's *The Bouviers* and *The Kennedy Clan: Dynasty and Disaster* (Sidgwick & Jackson, London, 1985); Charles Higham's *Rose: The Life and Times of Rose Fitzgerald Kennedy* (Pocket Books, 1999); Kitty Kelley's *Jackie Oh!* (Ballantine Books, 1979); Laurence Leamer's *The Kennedy Women;* Ralph G. Martin's *Seeds of Destruction: Joe Kennedy and His Sons* (Putnam, 1995); and Joan Meyers's *John Fitzgerald Kennedy . . . As We Remember Him* (Running Press, 1988).

II. AN INCONGRUOUS COUPLE

The description of Jackie's Christmas shopping, her attitude toward the Christmas holiday, her drive to New Jersey, her health concerns, and Maurice Tempelsman's attitude toward Jackie's health are based on the author's interviews with several friends of Jackie's who wish to remain anonymous.

Information about John Kennedy Jr.'s secret flying lessons comes from the author's sources in the insurance industry.

Maurice's warning to Jackie not to push John so hard comes from interviews with friends of Maurice who wish to remain anonymous. The quote "Jackie never used one of her favorite words . . ." comes from a friend of Jackie's who wishes to remain anonymous. Jackie's quote "Have you seen that photo of Daryl . . ." and the quote "John loved his mother . . ." are based on a conversation she had with one of her closest friends, who asked for anonymity.

Jackie's quotes "I want him to do something meaningful . . ." and "John has never shown the slightest interest . . ." were taken from the author's notes of conversations he had with Jackie.

The account of Maurice Tempelsman's background, business dealings, and developing relationship with Jackie was drawn from interviews with a number of friends and business associates of Tempelsman's who wish to remain anonymous.

In addition, the author interviewed Hélenè Arpels, Arnaud de Borchgrave, Frank Carlucci, Larry Devlin, Roy Furmark, Jeffrey Gartner, Brendan Gill, Brandon Grove, Robert Oakley, Michael G. Schatzberg, Sue Schmidt, Alex Shoumatoff, Adlai Stevenson Jr., Jack Valenti, Dr. Herbert Weiss, former New York mayor Ed Koch, Tillie Weitzner, John Loring, and Melissa Wells.

In an interview with the author, Rabbi Arthur Schneier discussed in general terms the legal requirement of a Jewish divorce, or get.

Other author interviews in this section were conducted with Michael Berman and Lou Adler.

The author also drew on accounts in periodicals for his description of Tempelsman's relationship with Jackie. These include the author's own cover story in the August 1989 issue of *Vanity Fair*, titled "Jackie, Yo!"; Paula Span's "The Man at Jackie's Side," *The Washington Post*, May 26, 1994; "The Man Who Loved Jackie," *People*, July 11, 1994; Jessie Mangaliman's "Jacqueline Kennedy Onassis—A City Mourns," *Newsday*, May 21, 1994; Sandra Sanchez's "Longtime Friend: 'Journey Is Over,'" *USA Today*, May 24, 1994; Susan Baer's "Jacqueline Kennedy Onassis: 1929–1994," *Los Angeles Times*, May 24, 1994; and Judith Thurman's "Costume of the Country," *The New Yorker*, May 14, 2001.

Periodical sources for the description of Tempelsman's business dealings in Africa and elsewhere include "Maurice Tempelsman's African Connections," *Fortune*, November 15, 1982; "Maurice Tempelsman: Diamonds and Diplomacy," *Jewelers' Circular Keystone*, June 1989; "To De Beers on Prices: Don't Kill Golden Goose," *Jewelers Circular Keystone*, September 1989 and August 1991; Vladimir Kvint's "Sorry Mr. Oppenheimer," *Forbes*, February 15, 1993; Rita Koselka's "Brand Name Diamonds?," *Forbes*, April 28, 1986; Leon Dash's "Zaire Gambles by Resigning Diamond Cartel," *The Washington Post*, November 11, 1981; Howard W. French's "In Africa, Wealth Often Buys Only Trouble," *The New York Times*, January 15, 1998; James Ring Adams's "Citizen Kennedy's Energy," *The American Spectator*, December 1997; "U.S. Diamond Dealer Turns Peacemaker," *Africa News*, August 15, 1997; John Elvin's "Angolan Angle," *The Washington Times*, September 20, 1990; Jim McGee's "Polishing Off a Ban on S. African Diamonds," *The Washington Post*, January 25, 1990; *The Orange County Register*, June 29, 1989; and the London *Mail on Sunday*, May 22, 1994.

Books that were used in this section include Jan Pottker's *Janet & Jackie: The Story of a Mother and Her Daughter, Jacqueline Kennedy Onassis* (St. Martin's Press, 2001); Carl Sferrazza Anthony's *As We Remember Her: Jacqueline Kennedy Onassis in the*

Words of Her Family and Friends (Perennial, 2003); Lester David's *Jacqueline Kennedy Onassis: A Portrait of Her Private Years;* C. David Heymann's *A Woman Named Jackie;* and Michael G. Schatzberg's *Mobutu or Chaos?* (Rowman & Littlefield, 1991).

Some of the material on John Marquand Jr., John Vernou Bouvier, and Aristotle Onassis appeared in a different form in the author's *Just Jackie.*

The description of Jackie's romantic entanglement with Marquand is drawn chiefly from interviews the author conducted with Marquand's friends, including George Plimpton, Peter Duchin, Cass Canfield Jr., and Thomas Guinzburg. Further interviews were conducted with Brigit Gurney; Nina Auchincloss Straight; and several sources who requested anonymity. Gore Vidal's *Palimpsest: A Memoir* (Penguin, 1996) contains a brief passage about Jackie's intimate relationship with Marquand.

For insight into Aristotle Onassis, the author drew on his interviews with Stelio Papadimitriou, Captain Costa Anastassiadis, and Niki Goulandris.

The quote from Samuel Pisar ("This thoughtful, unlikely . . .") and the quote from John Richardson ("A few years ago . . .") appeared in the author's August 1989 *Vanity Fair* article.

New York, New York, October 1965
(Twenty-nine years earlier)

This section is based on conversations the author had with Sydney Gruson.

Acapulco, Mexico, New Year's Eve, 1973
(Twenty-one years earlier)

This section is based on interviews the author conducted with Eleanor Lambert.

Otis Air Force Base Hospital and Boston Children's Hospital, Massachusetts, August 7–9, 1963 (Thirty years earlier)

This section is based on interviews with Dave Powers and Evelyn Lincoln that were originally done by the author for *All Too Human.*

III. THE ONUS OF THE DISEASE

The material in this section on Jackie's spiritual life is based on a half-dozen interviews with Catholic priests and nuns, most of whom spoke to the author on the condition of anonymity. One priest who did go on the record was Monsignor George Bardes of St. Thomas More Church.

The description of Jackie's apartment is drawn from the author's notes of his visits there.

The scene between Jackie and her children is based on conversations Caroline Kennedy Schlossberg and John F. Kennedy Jr. had with their friends, who spoke to the author.

For insight into Jackie's illness, the author relied on interviews with Lawrence K. Altman of *The New York Times,* Dr. Bernard Kruger, and several other physicians who treated Jackie and spoke with the author on condition of anonymity.

Arthur M. Schlesinger Jr.'s quote ("She said, 'I feel it is a kind of hubris . . .' ") has appeared in a number of books, including *Just Jackie.*

The author interviewed Natalia Aldea regarding Jackie's regular manicures and pedicures, and Jackie's attitude toward her grooming as she got sicker and sicker.

Books that were used in this section include Susan Sontag's *Illness as Metaphor & AIDS and Its Metaphors* (Picador USA, 2001).

Washington, D.C., January 15, 1964 (Thirty years earlier)

This section is based on an interview the author conducted with Robert McNamara for *Just Jackie.*

Lenox Hill Hospital, New York, Fall 1985 (Nine years earlier)

This section is based on an interview the author conducted for *Just Jackie* with a close friend of Maurice Tempelsman, who spoke on the condition of anonymity.

IV. THE SHOCK OF RECOGNITION

For contemporaneous information on Jackie's illness, the author relied on the following sources: *The Baltimore Sun,* February 16, 1994; *The New York Times,* February 11, 1994; and *Newsday,* February 12, 1994.

Books that were used in this section include Christopher Andersen's *Sweet Caroline;* the author's *All Too Human* and *Just Jackie;* and Laurence Leamer's *The Kennedy Women.*

For the scene of Jackie visiting the St. Thomas More Church on Ash Wednesday, the author relied on his interviews with Monsignor George Bardes.

The material on Caroline and her husband, Edwin Schlossberg, is based on interviews the author conducted with their friends, all of whom requested anonymity.

The author based his remarks about Jackie's superstitious nature on his personal observations and material that originally appeared in his book, *The Kennedy Curse: Why Tragedy Has Haunted America's First Family for 150 Years* (St. Martin's Press, 2003).

The description of the relationship between Jackie's children and Maurice Tempelsman comes from author interviews with friends of Caroline, John, and Maurice.

Casey Ribicoff spoke to the author about the dinner she and her husband, former senator Abraham Ribicoff, had with Jackie and Maurice.

For information on Jackie's professional life as an editor, the author relied on Aileen Mehle's "Suzy" column in *Women's Wear Daily*, as well as on interviews with John Loring, Gita Mehta, and Mark Hampton.

Peter Duchin supplied the author with information on Jackie's frame of mind during the period covered by this section.

V. HER ENDURING LEGACY

Information on Jackie's cancer treatment and her worsening physical health was provided by Niki Goulandris, Dr. James Nicholas, and several physicians who were acquainted with Jackie's course of treatment and who spoke to the author on condition of anonymity.

Books used in this section include Dr. Arthur Kleinman's *The Illness Narratives: Suffering, Healing & the Human Condition* (Basic Books, 1988); J. B. West and Mary L. Kotz's *Upstairs in the White House* (Warner Books, 1983); and David M. Lubin's *Shooting Kennedy: JFK and the Culture of Images* (University of California Press, 2003).

Periodicals used include Carl Sferrazza Anthony's "The Substance Behind the Style," *Town & Country*, July 1994; and Arthur M. Schlesinger Jr.'s "Jacqueline Kennedy in the White House," an essay that appeared in *Jacqueline Kennedy, the White House Years: Selections from the JFK Library and Museum*, edited by Hamish Bowles (Little, Brown, 2001).

The author conducted interviews with Paul Goldberger, John Carl Warnecke, Robert McNamara, Monsignor George Bardes, and Niki Goulandris.

Washington, D.C., Spring 1964 (Thirty years earlier)

This scene is based on reporting in Thomas Maier's book *The Kennedys: America's Emerald Kings* (Basic Books, 2003).

Martha's Vineyard, Massachusetts, August 1993 (Seven months earlier)

This section is based on an interview with Gus Ben David.

VI. MAKING A SMALL MASTERPIECE

The author Marie Brenner kindly made available several essays that Jackie submitted for *Vogue's* Prix de Paris contest in 1950. Ms. Brenner discovered the material in the *Vogue* archives during the course of her own research for an article she wrote for that magazine after Jackie's death. Excerpts from these documents were published in the author's *All Too Human.*

For an analysis of Jackie's last will and testament, the author drew heavily on "Lessons from the Will of Jacqueline Kennedy Onassis," by Susan E. Kuhn, which appeared in the July 11, 1994, issue of *Forbes.*

Several of Jackie's doctors told the author that they received books from Jackie, which she had specifically picked out for them before she died.

The scene of Jackie burning her letters was related to the author by an anonymous source who was in the room at the time.

The contents of John Carl Warnecke's letter to Jackie were revealed to the author by Mr. Warnecke.

Books that were used in this section include Christopher Andersen's *Sweet Caroline;* C. David Heymann's *A Woman Named Jackie;* the author's *All Too Human* and *Just Jackie;* Laurence Leamer's *The Kennedy Women;* and J. Randy Taraborrelli's *Jackie, Ethel, Joan.*

Jackie's habit of speaking freely and openly about some of the intimate details of her life to a few close friends comes from one of those friends, who requested anonymity.

The quote from Oleg Cassini ("It gradually dawned on her . . .") comes from an interview conducted by the author for *All Too Human.*

The quotes from Aaron Shikler ("I did many, many studies . . ."), Niki Goulandris ("As soon as Nancy Tuckerman . . ."), and Carly Simon ("When she got back to New York . . .") come from interviews conducted by the author.

The quote from Nancy Tuckerman ("With her flagrant imagination . . .") comes from Christopher Andersen's *Sweet Caroline.*

Jackie's quotes during her lunch at Carly Simon's apartment come from interviews the author conducted with people who attended the lunch and who requested anonymity.

The texts of Jackie's notes to John and Caroline have been printed in other books.

Hyannis Port, Massachusetts, November 1964
(Thirty years earlier)

Some of the material in this section, which is based on several interviews the author conducted with John Carl Warnecke, appeared in a different form in *Just Jackie.*

VII. HER WAY

Some of Jackie's doctors, nurses, and members of the New York Hospital staff agreed to speak to the author about Jackie's final days and hours on the condition of anonymity. They also described for the author the reactions of John and Caroline to their mother's suffering, and the death scene in Jackie's bedroom.

Information about Jackie's careful preparations for her own death was provided to the author by numerous sources, including Jackie's friends, members of her family, religious counselors, and health care professionals.

The Reverend Wallace Modrys provided insight into preparations by Jackie and the Kennedy family for her funeral. Monsignor George Bardes discussed with the author the reluctance of John and Caroline to accept their mother's condition as fatal and to allow the administration of the last rites of the Catholic Church.

Further details were provided in interviews conducted with Peter Duchin, Carly Simon, and others.

The brief conversation between Jackie and Ted Kennedy was described by someone who was in the room at the time and spoke to the author on condition of anonymity.

The quote from Eunice Shriver ("For us—and to my wonderful and big, extended family . . .") comes from Laurence Leamer's *The Kennedy Women.*

The description of the wake held in Jackie's apartment was provided by several sources, including Carly Simon, Monsignor George Bardes, and others who attended the wake and requested anonymity.

The description of Jackie's funeral is based on the author's personal observations. The Reverend Wallace Modrys and Aileen Mehle provided information about what transpired inside the church.

The author interviewed Mark Hampton regarding the sale of Jackie's apartment and the Sotheby's auction of her personal possessions.

In addition, the author interviewed Sue Erikson Bloland, Lisa DePaulo, Michael Beschloss, and David Pecker regarding the impact of Jackie's death on John.

Middleburg, Virginia, November 1993 (Six months earlier)

The Charles Whitehouse recollection of Jackie's quote ("Oh, not yet, Charlie . . .") comes from "Remembering Jackie . . . ," *Town & Country*, July 1994.

LIST OF PHOTOGRAPHS

p. 62   Jackie and Maurice, in an undated photograph, attend a black-tie dinner at the Waldorf-Astoria Hotel in New York. (© *Brian Quigley*)

p. 70   Jackie O with Ari at a Park Avenue party, 1971. (© *Sal Traina/WWD*)

p. 72   Famed paparazzo Ron Galella catches Jackie in an unguarded moment striding along Park Avenue. (© *1971 Ron Galella*)

p. 75   The President and First Lady leave Otis Air Force Base Hospital after the death of two-day-old Patrick Bouvier Kennedy, 1963. (© *Bettmann/Corbis*)

p. 81   A cardinal receives former First Lady Jacqueline Kennedy during her private audience with Pope Paul VI at the Vatican, 1966. (© *Hulton Archive/Getty Images*)

p. 86   JFK Jr. with his wife, Carolyn Bessette Kennedy. (© *Alexander/NYP/Globe Photos, Inc., 1996*)

p. 106   Jackie chats with her daughter, Caroline, on the deck of Maurice Tempelsman's yacht, *Relemar*, on Martha's Vineyard, 1993. (© *Dirck Halstead/Getty Images*)

p. 108   JFK Jr. listens to music while skating along the sidewalks of New York. (© *Laura Cavanaugh/Globe Photos, Inc.*)

p. 113   Jackie dresses for success as a book editor. (© *Alfred Eisenstaedt/Time Life Pictures/Getty Images*)

p. 119   A seriously ill Jackie with Maurice and Caroline (holding her son, Jack) in Central Park, 1994. (© *Bill Davila/Retna Ltd.*)

p. 138   Jackie testifies in favor of saving a landmark church during an appearance before state lawmakers in Albany, N.Y., 1984. (© *John Carl D'Annibale/Getty Images*)

p. 140   Pablo Cassals takes a bow after his performance at the Kennedy White House, 1962. (© *Cecil Stoughton, White House/John Fitzgerald Kennedy Library, Boston*)

p. 152   Jackie with architect John Carl Warnecke inspecting plans for the redesign of Lafayette Square, Washington, D.C., 1962. (© *Robert Knudsen, White House/John Fitzgerald Kennedy Library, Boston*)

p. 175   Carly Simon and Joe Armstrong, two of Jackie's closest friends, arrive at 1040 Fifth Avenue to pay their final respects to the dying former First Lady. (© *Rick Maiman/Corbis Sygma*)

p. 178   JFK Jr. announces to the media that his mother has died, May 20, 1994. (© *Luc Novovitch/AP/Wide World Photo*)

p. 185   Jackie's coffin is borne from St. Ignatuis Loyola Church after her funeral. (© *Andrea Renault/Globe Photos, Inc., © 1994*)

p. 193   Jackie plays with five-year-old Caroline in Hyannis Port, Massachusetts, 1962. (© *2000 Mark Shaw/MPTV.net*)